CAREERS IN SEARCH AND RESCUE OPERATIONS

CAREERS IN THE
COAST GUARD'S
SEARCH AND RESCUE UNITS

Greg Roza

the rosen publishing group's
**rosen
central**

In Memory of William J. McConnell

Published in 2003 by The Rosen Publishing Group, Inc.
29 East 21st Street, New York, NY 10010

Copyright © 2003 by The Rosen Publishing Group, Inc.

First Edition

Library of Congress Cataloging-in-Publication Data

Roza, Greg.
Careers in the Coast Guard's search and rescue unit / Greg Roza.
    p. cm. — (Careers in search and rescue operations)
Summary: Discusses the history of the Coast Guard's Search and Rescue units, requirements of becoming a member of one of these units, and the role Guardsmen played after the events of September 11, 2001.
Includes bibliographical references and index.
ISBN 978-1-4358-3641-9
1. United States. Coast Guard—Search and rescue operations—Juvenile literature. 2. United States. Coast Guard—Vocational guidance—Juvenile literature. [1. United States. Coast Guard—Vocational guidance.
2. Rescue work—Vocational guidance. 3. Vocational guidance.]
I. Title. II. Series.
VG53 .R69 2003
363.28'6—dc21

                                                                2002013263

Manufactured in the United States of America

CONTENTS

INTRODUCTION   Semper Paratus   4

CHAPTER 1   Coast Guard History   10

CHAPTER 2   The Coast Guard Today   22

CHAPTER 3   Search and Rescue   35

CHAPTER 4   True Stories   42

CHAPTER 5   How September 11, 2001,
                    Changed the Coast Guard   46

                Glossary   51

                For More Information   53

                For Further Reading   55

                Bibliography   57

                Index   61

INTRODUCTION

Semper Paratus

On the morning of September 11, 2001, two hijacked commercial airplanes crashed into the two towers of the World Trade Center in lower Manhattan. This event left many people feeling scared and vulnerable. Never before had terrorism of this magnitude reached American soil. As the day unfolded, U.S. armed forces sprang into action. Police officers, firefighters, emergency technicians, even construction workers and businesspeople rushed into the war zone to help however they could; tragically, many of those heroes lost their lives when the twin towers came crashing down. Despite the catastrophe that took place that morning, rescue workers demonstrated immense bravery, compassion, and skill.

Within minutes of the first attack, two Coast Guard helicopters stationed in Atlantic City, New Jersey, approached the scene, but they were unable to help because there was so much heavy smoke in the air. Two Coast Guard vessels from New York and New Jersey rushed in to evacuate the injured. They were soon joined by other Coast Guard ships, including a cutter (a small, fast ship) from Bayonne, New Jersey, and a buoy tender (a ship used to maintain buoys). The crew members on these ships rushed injured people to medical facilities that had been set up in Liberty State Park, New Jersey.

Throughout the day, the Coast Guard contributed to the rescue efforts in many other ways. A Coast Guard unit from Fort Dix, New Jersey, brought a mobile command post to the southern tip of Manhattan to aid the New York City Police Department. Another unit from Chesapeake, Virginia, flew a communications

In Nantucket, Massachusetts, four members of the U.S. Coast Guard return from a flight over the ocean after investigating the crash of an Egyptian airliner 60 miles (97 kilometers) offshore.

trailer in from Elizabeth City, North Carolina. The Coast Guard sent crew members, cutters, helicopters, and airplanes into the area to aid in the rescue mission. In addition, the Coast Guard called upon dozens of ships to help out, including an oil spill response vessel, ferries, tugboats, tour boats, cruise ships, and even privately owned boats. Between 10 AM on September 11 and 3 AM on September 12, the Coast Guard estimates that approximately one million people were evacuated from the southern tip of Manhattan.

The Coast Guard's participation did not end there. Before dawn on September 12, Coast Guard forces gathered in the waters around New York City and Washington, D.C., to secure ports. Helicopters from nearby cites were brought in to help transport people and supplies. Twelve Coast Guard cutters were soon on patrol in New York Harbor. Reservists and port security experts from as far away as St. Petersburg, Florida, were called in, and many others were put on alert. Coast Guard chaplains and stress management teams came to New York City to provide counseling for police officers, firefighters, and members of the armed forces. Coast Guard crews all over the United States patrolled and even shut down ports to ensure the safety of U.S. residents. Larger Coast Guard ships were positioned near major ports to protect the waterways. Despite all this activity, the Coast Guard continued to carry on with their day-to-day duties, which include patrolling for drug smugglers, protecting marine wildlife, and performing search and rescue missions.

On September 14, 2001, the U.S. Coast Guard cutter *Tahoma* tirelessly patrols New York Harbor. Even though it has been three days since the terrorist attacks on the World Trade Center, smoke still rises from the wreckage of the collapsed buildings.

Over the next few weeks, the Coast Guard continued to play a major role in cleaning up, providing protection, and preparing for a future that had become deeply uncertain. Two thousand Coast Guard reservists were activated on September 14 to help the regular Coast Guard do its job. Thirty-eight Coast Guard cutters were placed on patrol in New York Harbor. The Coast Guard heightened security in ports all over the nation, using cutters and aircraft to patrol the waters around them and carefully inspecting all incoming ships.

During its long history, the Coast Guard has developed into a diverse agency capable of responding to a variety of circumstances—large and small—with swift and precise action. For well over 100 years, the Coast Guard has used an ancient Latin phrase to describe the way they envision their job: *Semper Paratus*—"always ready."

No one is sure when this phrase became the Coast Guard's motto, but it was a Coast Guard captain named Francis Saltus Van Boskerck who penned the official Coast Guard anthem, "Semper Paratus," in 1922. Five years later, he wrote music to go with the words. Shortly after this, the phrase was added to the Coast Guard standard, or flag. Since then, the words of the anthem have been changed a little to reflect current times, but the new version remains true to the essence of Van Boskerck's original lyrics. The phrase Semper Paratus, the anthem based on that phrase, and the standard that bears those words have come to embody everything that the men and women of the Coast Guard value.

Coast Guard Anthem

"Semper Paratus"

Original words and music by Captain Francis Saltus
Van Boskerck, USCG
Copyright by Sam Fox Publishing Co., Inc.

From North and South and East and West,
The Coast Guard's in the fight.
Destroying subs and landing troops,
The Axis feels our might.
For we're the first invaders,
On every fighting field.
Afloat, ashore, on men and Spars,
You'll find the Coast Guard shield.

We're always ready for the call,
We place our trust in Thee.
Through howling gale and shot and shell,
To win our victory.
"Semper Paratus" is our guide,
Our pledge, our motto, too.
We're "Always Ready," do or die!
Aye! Coast Guard, we fight for you.

CHAPTER 1

Coast Guard History

The Coast Guard's past is an adventure story. It is inspiring, terrifying, and sometimes surprising. The fact of the matter is that the Coast Guard was originally part of the U.S. Treasury. The treasury controls our money—they make it, keep track of it, collect it during tax season, and enforce the federal laws regarding it. How does the Coast Guard fit in? It's an interesting story.

Early Origins

On January 14, 1784, the American Revolution ended. American citizens were no longer English colonists; they had earned their independence. The war, however, had left the infant country with very little money. The U.S. government was in need of funds to keep the new nation afloat. In order to raise money, Congress and the treasury of the United States taxed all goods coming into the United States from other countries. This was a desperate yet necessary move for the new government. British taxes had been one of the reasons that the colonists fought in the American Revolution, and few Americans wanted to pay taxes they thought were unfair.

During the war, many smugglers became heroes by outrunning British ships and sneaking goods into the colonies. After the war, these same smugglers were expected to pay tariffs on incoming goods. Most smugglers continued to sneak goods into the colonies. The leaders of the nation realized that something had to be done to enforce the new tariff laws.

President George Washington appointed Alexander Hamilton as the first secretary of the treasury. It was Hamilton's job to

The Coast Guard cutter *Manhattan*, built in 1872, patrols New York Harbor. It was transferred to the U.S. Navy after the start of the United States's involvement in World War II.

manage America's money. It was also his job to raise money for the country. Hamilton had to make some quick decisions regarding the smugglers and the lost revenue. He asked Congress for ten cutters to patrol the shores of the new nation and search for smugglers. He hoped to enforce the tariff laws and to raise more money for the United States.

On August 4, 1790, the Coast Guard was officially established, but it wasn't called the Coast Guard. This new agency was known by several names, including Reserve Cutters, Revenue Service, and Revenue Marine. The ten small cutters were required to patrol 2,000 miles (604 kilometers) of coastline. While there were probably people who thought Hamilton had wasted a little more than $10,000 by starting the Revenue Service, the brave, hardworking crews of the cutters did their best to prove them wrong. In the first ten years, the revenue that was collected on imports and exports rose from $52 million to $205 million.

Other Law Enforcement Duties

As the Revenue Service grew, they began to chase and apprehend pirates who preyed on honest (and dishonest) shipping companies. From 1794 until 1861 when the American Civil War began, the Coast Guard was responsible for preventing ships carrying African slaves from reaching the shores of the United States. During that time, the Coast Guard arrested many people who were involved in the foreign slave trade and freed about 500 slaves.

The Coast Guard has also been responsible for seizing illegal contraband. In 1920, Congress added the Eighteenth Amendment to the U.S. Constitution, which prohibited the manufacture, sale, transportation, import, and export of alcohol. During this time in American history (which became known as Prohibition), Coast Guard ships chased down and even sunk ships trying to bring alcohol into the United States. In recent years, the Coast Guard has focused its energies on drug smugglers trying to bring illegal drugs into the United States.

The Many Faces of the Coast Guard

The Coast Guard that we know today is a combination of several government agencies, each with a connection to maritime concerns. Through the years, these agencies were merged to form a single agency called the Coast Guard. In addition to law enforcement, the Coast Guard is also responsible for national defense, homeland security, protection of environmental resources, maritime search and rescue, freeing international and domestic waters from ice, maintaining navigational aids (lighthouses and buoys, for example), port security, and boating safety.

Lighthouses and Lightships

Before the Revenue Service was founded in 1790, there was a system of lighthouses and lightships (traveling lighthouses) in place to aid ships that were navigating at night and during stormy weather. In August 1789, America's new government created an agency to maintain lighthouses, buoys, and beacons that had been built by the colonies. This agency was called the Lighthouse Service.

Lighthouse keepers were often highly praised for their bravery. They had to stay at their stations for long periods of time, most often at night and during poor weather. Many women have served as lighthouse keepers since 1789. In fact, between 1828 and 1947, 138 women were employed as lighthouse keepers.

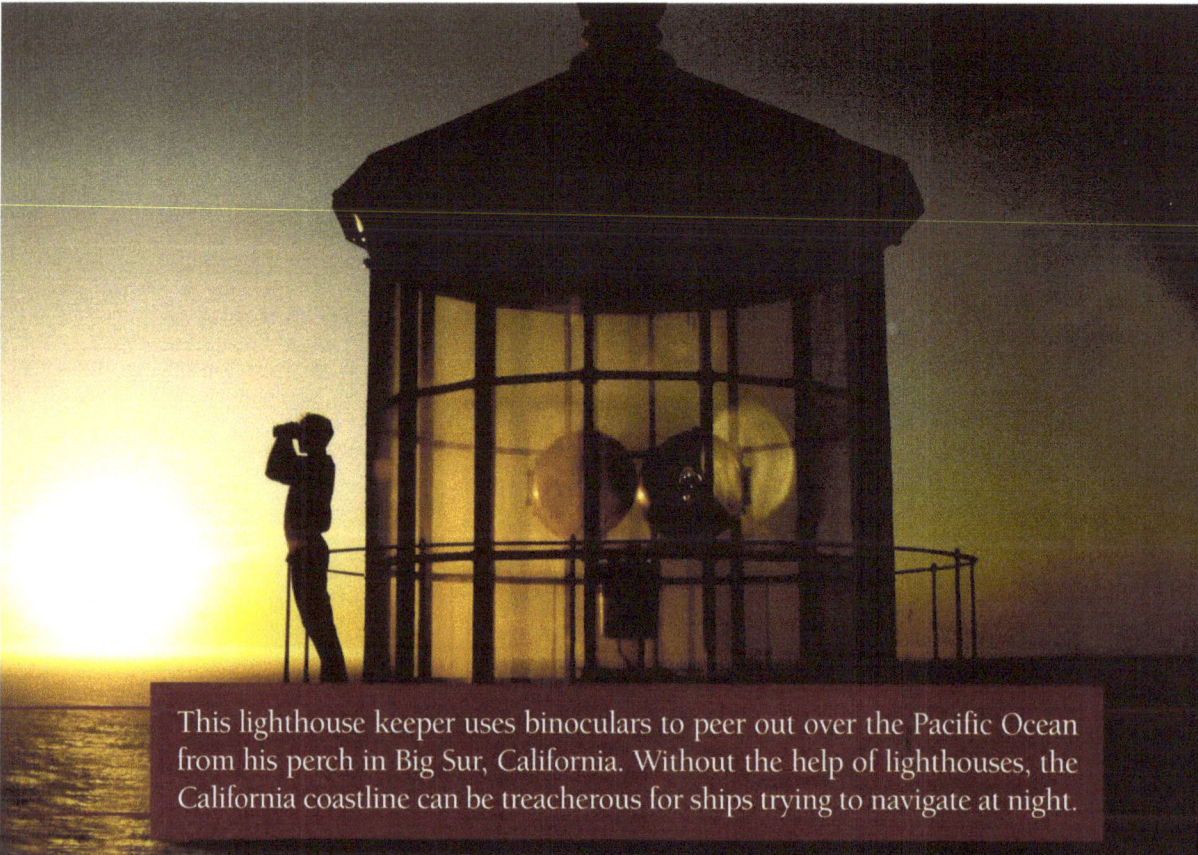

This lighthouse keeper uses binoculars to peer out over the Pacific Ocean from his perch in Big Sur, California. Without the help of lighthouses, the California coastline can be treacherous for ships trying to navigate at night.

Lightships have played a similar role in keeping American waters safe for ships. They kept watch in locations where it wasn't possible to build lighthouses. The first lightship patrolled the waters of Chesapeake Bay in 1820. Since then, there have been more than 120 lightships. Manning a lightship was a dangerous job. Many were sunk during storms or because of collisions with other ships. Today, lightships have been replaced by buoys that mark frequently traveled routes. However, lighthouses still play an important role in maritime safety and navigation.

Military

If you were to ask, most Coasties (as members of the Coast Guard are called) would probably say that as a branch of the military, the Coast Guard does not receive the same respect that the other branches receive. However, the Coast Guard has participated in nearly every American conflict since the United States became a country.

The Coast Guard is the oldest of the five branches of the U.S. military (Army, Navy, Air Force, Marines, and Coast Guard). The Continental navy, which had fought in the American Revolution, broke apart at the end of the war. Between 1790 and 1798, the Revenue Service was the only agency that protected American shores. The U.S. Navy was established in 1798 to help protect Americans at home and abroad. The Coast Guard continued to police the waters around America and protect American shores, but it also had a new responsibility: to aid the navy in times of war and at any other time that the president thought it necessary.

The first war in which the Coast Guard participated was a small war against French privateers in the Caribbean Sea from 1798 to 1799. It was the War of 1812, however, that helped to establish the Coast Guard's value as a military branch. Naval forces took advantage of the Coast Guard's small, quick cutters, which could outrun enemies close to the shore and along river routes. Since the War of 1812, the Coast Guard has fought in the Mexican War (1846–1848), the American Civil War (1861–1865), the Spanish-American War (1898–1899), World War I (1914–1918), World War II (1939–1945), the Korean War (1950–1953), the Vietnam War (1957–1975), and the Persian Gulf War (1990–1991).

In light of recent events, homeland security has become one of the most important responsibilities of the U.S. Coast Guard, perhaps even the most important. Historically, the Coast Guard has been protecting U.S. citizens since its earliest days. The people in the United States have been very fortunate; since the American Civil War, there has not been a major war fought on American soil. In part, the reason for this is because America is protected by two very large oceans. The U.S. military, and the Coast Guard specifically, have worked hard over the past 200 years to ensure against a foreign invasion by securing ports, patrolling waters, and investigating potentially threatening situations.

Environmental Protection

In 1822, Congress established a naval timber reserve (a forest where trees are grown to be used for building ships and other items). The Coast Guard was immediately placed in charge of protecting this reserve.

In 1867, the United States purchased Alaska from Russia. Seal hunting had become a problem in Alaska, and seals were in danger of extinction; approximately 250,000 seals were killed in the first four years after the United States purchased Alaska. In 1894, the Coast Guard set up a base in Alaska so that they could stop the illegal hunting of seals for their furs.

In 1885, the Coast Guard once again expanded their duties to include the protection of marine animals. The Coast Guard has enforced the laws regarding offshore fishing since that time. Since the early 1970s, the primary environmental duty of the Coast Guard has been combating pollution, especially oil spills.

Boating Safety and Inspection

Robert Fulton invented the steamboat in 1807. As steamboat travel grew more popular in the following years, boiler explosions became a serious problem. In 1837, a steamboat in North Carolina exploded, killing 100 people. This catastrophe prompted the federal government to create steamboat safety laws, and a new agency, the Steamboat Inspection Service, was entrusted with enforcing them. However, the laws were not that

Sinbad the Coast Guard Dog

One of the most famous Coast Guardsmen of all time wasn't human. Sinbad was a mutt adopted as the mascot of the Coast Guard cutter *Campbell* in 1937. Sinbad was a full-fledged member of the Coast Guard. He had his own bunk, his own specially made life preserver, and his own seat in the mess hall. He had even filled out his own enlistment papers (with a little help, of course).

During World War II, Sinbad crossed the equator several times, visited the Arctic, and crossed the international date line aboard the *Campbell*. The *Campbell* had been involved in numerous battles in the North Atlantic. By the end of the war, Sinbad had earned five ribbons of valor, just like the rest of the crew of the *Campbell*.

During his life, Sinbad "signed" autographs, was the subject of countless newspaper articles, appeared on television, and had a popular biography written about him titled *Sinbad of the Coast Guard*. Sinbad even starred in his own Hollywood movie in 1947, *Dog of the Seven Seas*.

In 1948, Sinbad retired from the *Campbell* and was assigned to the Coast Guard Lighthouse Station at Barnegat, New Jersey. There, he helped the crew watch for ships in danger. Sinbad passed away in 1951, after fifteen years as a dedicated member of the Coast Guard.

effective because no inspection standards were established, and each inspector used his own judgment on the safety of a steamship. As a result, in 1852, the Steamboat Inspection Act was passed, which helped to cut down on unsafe steamboats even though some problems still existed. Over the next fifty years, steamboat safety improved as safety regulations became even more strict and the Steamboat Inspection Service supplied their vessels with better fire fighting equipment.

The only Coast Guard member to be the subject of a biography, Sinbad (*left*) loyally served aboard the Coast Guard cutter *Campbell* for eleven years and even saw combat during World War II.

As recreational boating became popular, new laws were needed to fight the rising numbers of injuries and deaths that resulted from unsafe boating. In 1910, Congress passed the Motorboat Act, which made lights, whistles, fire extinguishers, and life preservers necessary boating equipment. In 1939, the Coast Guard Auxiliary was founded to further aid the regular Coast Guard in keeping boaters safe. Thanks to improved technology and stricter laws, the Coast Guard has effectively reduced the number of boating-related accidents.

Search and Rescue

The Coast Guard's search and rescue duties originated in 1831, when the secretary of the treasury authorized the use of one reserve cutter for the purpose of patrolling for ships and crews in danger. It wasn't until 1848, however, that a true lifesaving service began to come together. The government began to provide more effective equipment and storage facilities for search and rescue cutters. In 1871, the U.S. government officially funded the Life-Saving Service, which saved people from shipwrecks that occurred close to shore. More stations were built all along the East Coast of the United States, and new technology increased the success rate of lifesaving missions. Potential accidents were reduced because of improved navigational aids and better-constructed ships, but the drastic increase in the number of ships on the water made search and rescue missions crucial to maritime safety.

The twentieth century brought numerous innovations to search and rescue operations. Helicopters and amphibious aircraft (planes with floating devices that could land safely on water) made rescues quicker and more successful. The Coast Guard developed stations in the Atlantic Ocean and the Gulf of Mexico. Similarly, the Coast Guard developed a deepwater program with ships and aircraft that could operate for extended periods of time far out at sea. This allowed the Coast Guard to respond to distress calls far away from land. In the last thirty years, improved electronic equipment, computers, and communications technology have aided the Coast Guard in rescuing boaters in danger.

The Coast Guard Takes Shape

In 1915, the Revenue Service merged with the Life-Saving Service, forming a single agency called the Coast Guard that was responsible for patrolling U.S. waters and performing search and rescue missions. In the years following this merger, other agencies joined the Coast Guard, including the Lighthouse Service, the Steamboat Inspection Service, and the Bureau of Navigation.

Since 1967, the Coast Guard has been governed by the Department of Transportation in times of peace. In times of war, the Coast Guard is transferred to the Department of Defense. This demonstrates the flexibility that makes the United States Coast Guard a truly unique organization.

CHAPTER 2

The Coast Guard Today

Members of the Coast Guard have the chance to learn just about all there is to know about sailing and modern vessels. Similar to the other branches of the military, the Coast Guard is a great place to receive on-the-job training in a variety of professions: law enforcement, marine science, communications, electronics, and even food preparation and music. The Coast Guard offers more than just job training. When you enlist in any of the branches of the military, your first obligation is that of protecting your country. As with all U.S. military organizations, interested candidates must possess a strong desire to work hard and must be courageous when called upon.

Signing Up for the Coast Guard

Coast Guard boot camp is held in Cape May, New Jersey. Despite the fact that the Coast Guard is part of the Department of Transportation during times of peace, recruits can expect to take part in military training. Basic training usually lasts about eight weeks and involves hard physical exercise, classroom instruction, and specialized training sessions. Specialized training may include using ropes and tying knots, learning seamanship, and using a 9 mm handgun, for example. Once basic training is finished, new recruits are assigned to a station or ship. On-the-job training begins at this point. There is a wide range of jobs in the Coast Guard, from radar operator to law enforcement investigator, from marine science technician to weapons specialist.

Members of the Coast Guard are paid a monthly salary. New recruits make about $1,000 a month; newly commissioned officers make about $2,000. The salary depends on your level of experience and the amount of time you've been an enlisted member of the Coast Guard. While these numbers may seem somewhat low, enlisted individuals also receive generous benefits: yearly pay raises, free room and board, clothing expenditures, recreational allowances, free medical and dental care, retirement benefits, thirty days paid vacation every year, and college tuition for those who have been honorably discharged from the military.

Like the other branches of the military, you can learn more about the Coast Guard and basic training from your local recruiter. (Check the government listings in your local phone book to find the Coast Guard recruiter in your area.)

Coast Guard Academy

The Coast Guard Academy, located in New London, Connecticut, is a college for Coast Guard officers. Cadets who make it into the academy receive a full four-year scholarship and will earn a bachelor's degree in science by the time they finish. As in most colleges, the educational experience at the academy includes classroom training, athletics, internships, and leadership exercises. There are also music programs, a student government, and campus clubs. Upon graduation, each cadet becomes an ensign (the lowest rank

Although approximately 6,000 men and women apply to the Coast Guard Academy each year, only about 900 are accepted. Graduates will go on to serve proudly in the U.S. Coast Guard.

of commissioned officer) and is required to serve at least five years in the U.S. Coast Guard.

The majority of new cadets are in the top 25 percent of their graduating high school class. For those individuals willing to work hard and get good grades, it is one of the best ways to become an officer in the U.S. Coast Guard.

Coast Guard Reserves

The reserves are designed to enlarge the U.S. military forces in times of war. Reservists are required to attend training sessions one weekend a month and one week every year. When they are needed, reservists are called to active duty and join full-time members of the military in protecting the United States.

The Coast Guard Reserve was founded in 1941, after the United States joined World War II. Pay for new reservists is relatively low (about $130 for each weekend of training), but it increases the longer you are in the reserves and the higher your rank. The reserves also offer various benefits, such as signing bonuses and tuition packages. (To learn more about the Coast Guard Reserves, go to the URL listed on page 54.)

Coast Guard Auxiliary

The Coast Guard depends on volunteers to help educate citizens about boating laws and safety. This group of volunteers—

Coast Guard Ranks

Seaman Recruit (boot camp)
Seaman Apprentice (training and testing)
Seaman

Noncommissioned Officers (NCOs)

Petty Officer, 3rd Class
Petty Officer, 2nd Class
Petty Officer, 1st Class (may proceed to Commissioned Officer from here or continue in NCO ranks)
Chief Petty Officer (CPO-1)
Senior Chief Petty Officer (CPO-2)
Master Chief Petty Officer (CPO3)

Commissioned Officers

Chief Warrant Officer (CWO-1 through CWO-4)

Commissioned Officers from Academy or OCS (Officer Candidate School) Graduates

Ensign (O-1)
Lieutenant-JG (O-2)
Lieutenant (O-3)
Lieutenant Commander (O-4)
Commander (O-5)
Captain(O-6)
Rear Admiral (O-7)
Vice Admiral (O-8)
Admiral (O-9)
Admiral (O-10) (Commandant of U.S. Coast Guard)

approximately 33,000 of them—makes up the Coast Guard Auxiliary. After proper Coast Guard training, members of the Auxiliary can be called upon to help complete numerous tasks such as boating safety classes, navigational aid mainte-nance, safety examinations, radio watch at Coast Guard stations, recruiting, and search and rescue operations.

Women in the Coast Guard

Women have played important roles in the Coast Guard since its beginning, most notably as lighthouse keepers. On November 23, 1942, women were officially allowed to enlist in the U.S. Coast Guard as reservists. The U.S. government finally acknowledged that women had much to offer to the country as Coast Guardswomen. However, there were still obstacles for women to overcome at this point—female members of the Coast Guard could not serve overseas, for instance, and they could not issue orders to male members of the Coast Guard.

During World War II, many female members of the Coast Guard served their country as radar operators and LORAN (Long Range Aid to Navigation) technicians (for more information on LORAN, see page 34). After World War II, nearly all the women were phased out of the Coast Guard Reserves even though the other branches of the military continued to employ women.

It wasn't until 1973 that women were allowed to work side by side with men in the regular Coast Guard. This was also the year that the Coast Guard allowed women to become officers; the Coast Guard was the first branch of the military to do this. By 1978, all career fields within the Coast Guard—including positions on warships—were open to women. Today, women make up approximately 10 percent of the total members of the Coast Guard.

What Does the Coast Guard Do?

That's not an easy question to answer simply because the Coast Guard does so much. The Coast Guard has a long tradition of patrolling neighboring waters in order to enforce U.S. laws, especially laws relating to tariffs, to pirates, and to transporting contraband. Coast Guard law enforcement has extended to cover ship construction, boat inspections, pollution, the fishing industry, and the stopping of illegal aliens entering the country. Law enforcement, however, is only one aspect of Coast Guard activity. As the Coast Guard grew, so did its responsibilities.

Wartime Duties

The Coast Guard has two basic duties in times of war: to help the U.S. Navy by supplying it with men, women, and cutters; and to complete tasks with the skills specifically developed by the Coast Guard in times of peace, such as protecting America's coastlines.

In past wars, the Coast Guard has been used to patrol domestic waters, guard ports, capture or destroy enemy ships, escort and defend military and nonmilitary ships in foreign waters, and transport troops and equipment to locations all over the world. During World War II, Coast Guard ships sank a total of eleven Nazi submarines, including one that was rammed by the U.S. Coast Guard cutter *Campbell*.

Peacetime Duties

There are differences between the Coast Guard and the U.S. Army, Navy, Air Force, and Marines. Those branches of the military are exactly that—branches of the military. The Coast Guard, however, is a military organization with unique peacetime responsibilities. The sections that follow will address the peacetime duties of the Coast Guard.

Homeland Security

Homeland security—or the protection of people and property from hostile forces on U.S. soil—was thrust into the spotlight immediately after the tragic events of September 11, 2001. However, homeland security is not a new responsibility for the Coast Guard. The Coast Guard (or the agencies that would eventually become the Coast Guard) has protected the United States since the organization was founded.

The United States has more than 361 ports and about 95,000 miles (approximately 152,887 km) of coastline. It is a monumental task to protect these areas day in and day out. The Coast Guard works to keep transportation and commerce flowing smoothly while guarding U.S. borders against potential disasters. It is also responsible for making sure that the United States can quickly deploy military resources should the need arise. In essence, the Coast Guard is the first line of defense.

Boating Safety, Inspection, and Regulations

The Coast Guard regulates recreational boaters and boating areas similar to the way traffic officers regulate motorists and motorways. In 1971, Congress enacted the Federal Boat Safety Act to reduce the number of boating accidents that occur each year. In addition to providing safety instruction to recreational boaters, the Coast Guard also conducts inspections of private, passenger, and fishing vessels to make sure that they are safe to operate.

Since 1971, the number of recreational boats in U.S. waters has increased more than 100 percent, but the number of deaths resulting from boating accidents has fallen from 1,754 in 1971 to 701 in 2000. Despite the enormous improvement, the Coast Guard is still concerned; even one fatality is too many.

The Coast Guard Auxiliary conducts the Vessel Safety Check program. This is a free service provided by volunteer workers who check safety equipment on boats. They also supply boaters with information about the use of safety equipment.

The Coast Guard plays an important role in maintaining the safety of U.S. passenger ships. They oversee the design, construction, and operation of all passenger vessels. The Coast Guard also inspects fishing ships and trains their crews in safety procedures.

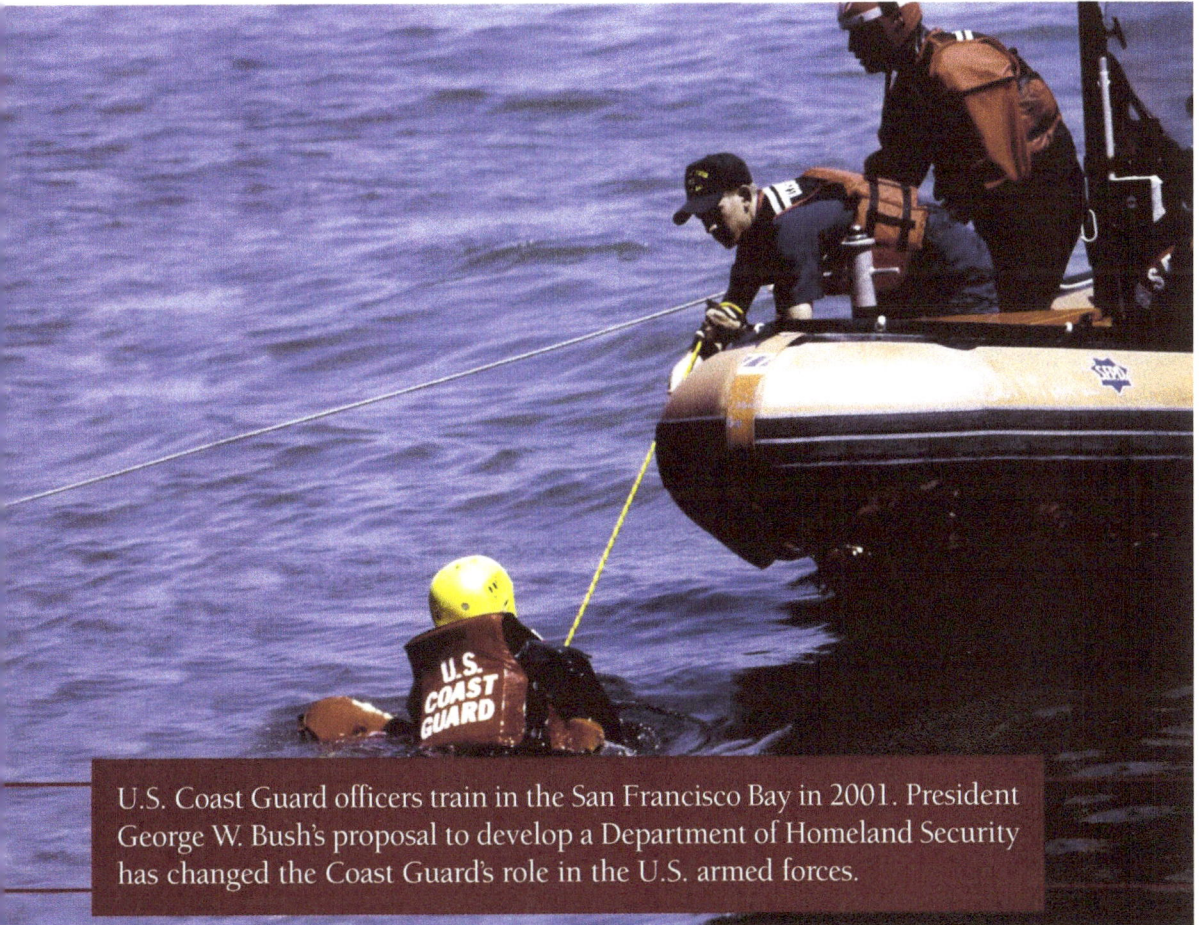

U.S. Coast Guard officers train in the San Francisco Bay in 2001. President George W. Bush's proposal to develop a Department of Homeland Security has changed the Coast Guard's role in the U.S. armed forces.

Environmental Protection

The Coast Guard helps to protect natural resources. Water pollution is an increasingly problematic issue, especially pollution resulting from oil spills. The Coast Guard does several things to prevent oil spills. They educate organizations and the crews of large oil tankers about the dangers of oil spills, enforce the laws pertaining to ships that carry large amounts of oil, and regularly inspect oil tankers to make sure that they are safe. In the instances when oil spills do occur, the Coast Guard has developed a rapid response cleanup team to combat environmental damage. These steps help the United States save billions of dollars a year.

Fishing is a significant U.S. business, and fishers run the risk of taking too many fish from U.S. waters. The Coast Guard enforces domestic and international fishery laws to ensure that we do not deplete our resources. They protect marine wildlife, such as seals and turtles, from hunters and natural predators. Foreign vessels are inspected before unloading to make sure that they do not contain species or bacteria that would be harmful to the native wildlife.

International Ice Patrol and Ice Breaking

In 1912, the RMS *Titanic*—the largest ocean liner ever built at the time—collided with an iceberg in the North Atlantic, resulting in the death of about 1,500 people. This event prompted countries on both sides of the Atlantic to gather to discuss safety in the transatlantic shipping lanes between Europe and North America. As of 1914, the U.S. Revenue Service, under orders from President Woodrow Wilson, established the International Ice Observation and Ice Patrol Service. Since then, the Coast Guard has used cutters and aircraft to patrol the Atlantic near Newfoundland in search of dangerous icebergs.

The headquarters for the International Ice Patrol Observation and Ice Patrol Service is located in Groton, Connecticut. The radar aircraft used for ice patrol are stationed in Elizabeth City, North Carolina. Since 1913, in the area monitored by the International Ice Observation and Ice Patrol, no lives or property have been lost as the result of iceberg collisions.

The Coast Guard is also responsible for keeping domestic and international shipping lanes free of ice with the help of ships called ice breakers. Ice breakers are large vessels that are strong enough to carve paths through shipping lanes blocked with ice. The Revenue Service began using ice breakers in 1867, when the United States purchased the state of Alaska from Russia. Since then, ice breakers have been used from San Francisco to Alaska, and from Chesapeake Bay to Greenland.

Aids to Navigation

It is the Coast Guard's job to make traveling in U.S. waters as easy and safe as possible. This means setting up and maintaining navigational aids. Today, there are 594 functioning lighthouses in the

United States. The Coast Guard also uses buoys, beacons, foghorns, and weather forecasting to help ships find their way.

Modern technology has improved navigational aids. The first significant technological improvements in navigational aids were radio communication (invented in 1895) and telephones (invented in 1876). Two monumental navigational aids were developed during World War II: radar and LORAN. Radar is used to locate an object by bouncing radio waves off of it. LORAN is similar to but more accurate than radar. It also uses radio waves to pinpoint a specific location. Today, there are LORAN stations all over the world, and the Coast Guard uses them extensively. The Coast Guard also uses a technology called global positioning system, or GPS. GPS uses computers and satellites to determine an exact location on Earth.

Lifesaving

Of all the Coast Guard's responsibilities, perhaps none is more noble than search and rescue. Lifesaving missions are selfless struggles to ensure the safety of others while risking one's own life. Without Coast Guard search and rescue teams, recreational boaters, commercial shippers, fishery employees, and many others would have little or no hope of rescue after a disaster at sea. The next two chapters will take a closer look at the lifesaving responsibilities of the U.S. Coast Guard.

CHAPTER 3

Search and Rescue

At 3:35 AM, a call goes out at the search and rescue station: "Mayday! Mayday! Mayday! Our ship is going down!" As an officer listens to the call coming over the radio, a small crew of seamen rush to the 47-foot (14.3-meter) lifeboat prepared for this moment. They receive directions and speed out into a cold, rainy night. The waves are fierce, and the small vessel rocks dangerously as it rushes out to answer the distress call. Lightning flashes in the distance and sporadic fog banks obstruct the pilot's vision, but still they race on. Most experienced boaters would not be caught outside on a night like this, let alone on the water. The Coast Guard search and rescue team, however, won't let bad weather sway them from their sworn duty: to search out and rescue people in danger.

"So That Others May Live"

Search and rescue operations are one of the oldest functions of the U.S. Coast Guard. The original search and rescue agency, the Life-Saving Service, was founded in 1871, and it officially merged with the Revenue Service to form the Coast Guard in 1915. Since then, search and rescue units have continually sought ways to improve their success in rescuing people.

The first search and rescue vessels were small cutters propelled with oars, which, in many situations, were unable to rescue

The Coast Guard responds to a call about a downed pontoon plane near Washougal, Washington, on the Columbia River. Coast Guard divers search for the bodies of the plane's four passengers.

people on ships that had been torn apart by treacherous weather and turbulent coastal waters. Over the years, technical innovations helped to improve the Coast Guard's ability to save lives at sea. These innovations started with sturdier ships and rescue stations, and were followed by harpoonlike tools used to cast lines out to people and ships in danger, motorized vessels, powerful lights, radios, radar, amphibious airplanes and helicopters, and computers. Lifesaving techniques have also changed, as in the case of rescue swimmers.

One thing that has remained the same is that search and rescue teams put their lives on the line to save the lives of others. They rush into danger when there is no one else to do so. This trait is the basis for the motto uttered by search and rescue teams all over the world: "So that others may live."

Coast Guard Vessels

All boats (vessels under 65 feet [19.8 m] in length) and cutters (those over 65 feet [19.8 m]) may be used for search and rescue missions. These include swift motorboats, buoy tenders, law enforcement patrol boats, ice breakers, tugboats, and large, high-endurance cutters. Small, fast, and powerful surfboats are needed to rescue people who are trapped in rough waters close to shore. The small boats allow the Coast Guard to get in and get out quickly. An ice breaker might be needed to reach people in Arctic or wintry environments. Large cutters may be used for deepwater rescue missions.

Aircraft and Helicopters

Aircraft and helicopters also play important roles in the day-to-day affairs of search and rescue operations. Such aircraft can often reach a vessel in distress faster than a cutter or motorboat. Amphibious planes can land on water near vessels in danger and take people to safety. Jets can travel long distances in a short amount of time.

The helicopter was developed by the Coast Guard during World War II to combat submarines. Later, the helicopter was worked into the search and rescue program. Helicopters, armed and unarmed, can travel long distances in a short amount of time and are vital in rescuing boaters from perilous conditions. A helicopter can hover over a specified area, lower a rescuer into the water, pluck a drowning person from the water, and rush injured boaters to medical facilities miles away.

Modern Technology

Technological advances have also allowed the Coast Guard to improve their ability to rescue people. Computers, communications systems, radar, LORAN, and GPS all play important roles in locating boaters in danger. At the time of the publication of this book, the Coast Guard is in the process of updating its fleet of vessels and aircraft, many of which are thirty and forty years old. New and improved ships will increase the Coast Guard's ability to respond quickly during search and rescue missions. The newest rescue vessel is a 47-foot (14.3-meter) motor lifeboat that is faster and sturdier than older Coast Guard vessels. In addition, it can withstand near-hurricane gusts, navigate 20-foot (6-meter) waves, and can right itself if it tips over during stormy weather.

The Canadian Coast Guard's fleet of icebreakers keeps ship routes open when the northern coastal waters freeze. An icebreaker's control room, pictured here, is equipped with sophisticated radar and computer technology.

Rescue Swimmers

The helicopter made rescuing capsized boaters quicker and easier than it had ever been before. A basket could be lowered to someone in danger, and that person could be raised to safety in very little time. However, there were still problems that needed to be solved. Rough waters make it impossible for amphibious helicopters to land. Also, the colder the water, the

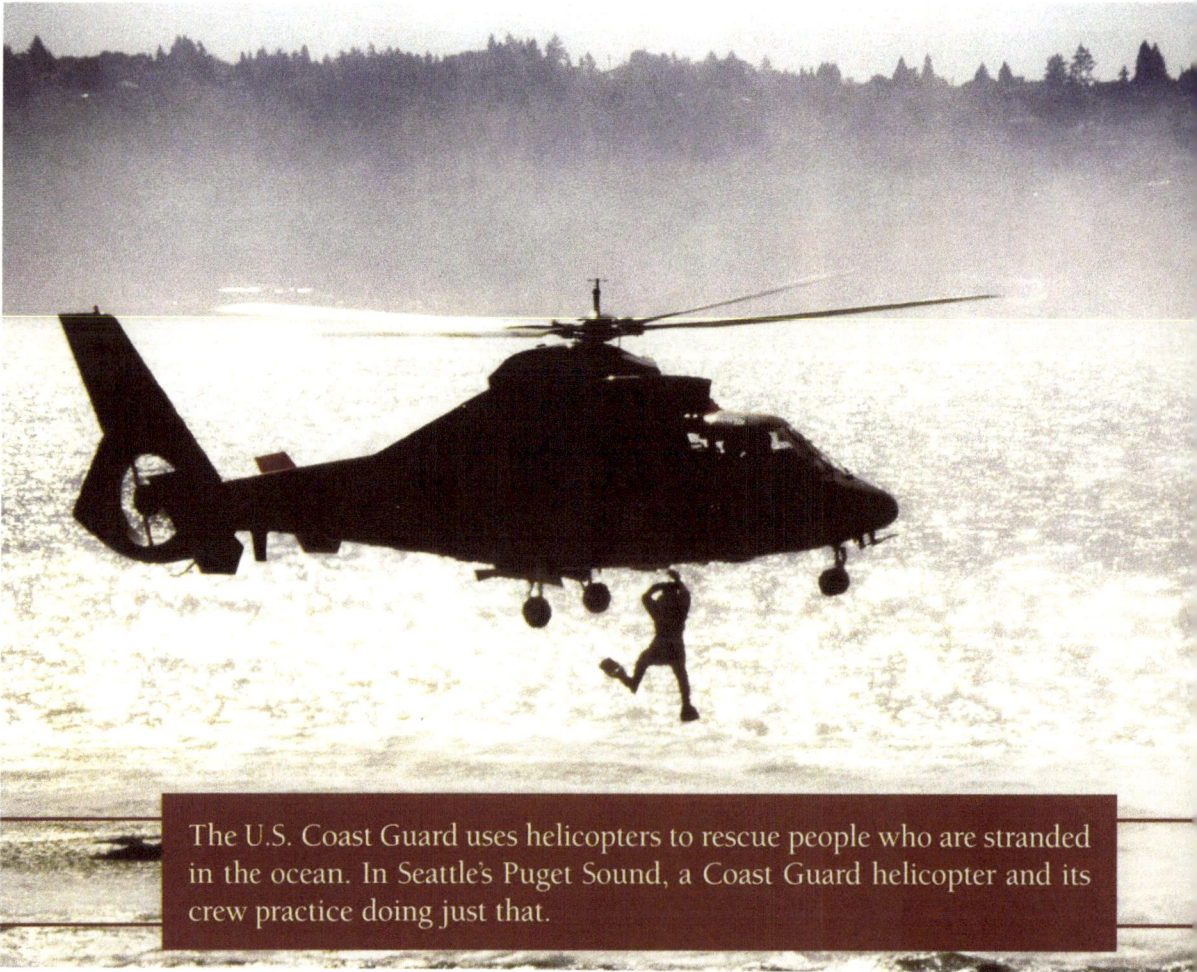

The U.S. Coast Guard uses helicopters to rescue people who are stranded in the ocean. In Seattle's Puget Sound, a Coast Guard helicopter and its crew practice doing just that.

less time victims have until hypothermia (low body temperature) sets in. Hypothermia greatly reduces the time available for rescue because it depletes a person's strength, numbs their limbs, and renders them unconscious.

In 1982, a ship named the *Marine Electric* sank off the coast of Virginia. The Coast Guard was quick to respond, but the waters were rough and freezing cold, and it was nearly impossible to help the thirty-four crew members who quickly succumbed to hypothermia. Helicopters lowered rescue baskets, but the men were too cold and tired to climb into them. Thirty-one members of the crew perished in the icy waters.

This tragedy may have been avoided if a rescue swimmer had been present that day. A rescue swimmer—wearing a thermal suit and swim fins—can be lowered into the cold water to help people into rescue baskets. Nine years after the *Marine Electric* tragedy, rescue swimmers became a part of every Coast Guard air station. By January 2001, Coast Guard rescue swimmers had saved more than 4,000 people.

CHAPTER 4

True Stories

Search and rescue is a complex job, one that can be calm one day and turbulent the next, or fulfilling one day and tragically sad the next. Only true stories of Coast Guard search and rescue can appropriately convey the intricate nuances of this demanding yet rewarding profession.

Terror on the Ice

The following true story was described in the book *Lifeboat Sailors* by retired Coast Guard senior chief Dennis L. Noble.

On February 10, 1996, Petty Officer Jeffery Kihlmire was stationed in Charlevoix, Michigan. That evening, freezing rain turned to snow and high winds by nightfall. Kihlmire's station soon got a call from someone who had heard a desperate voice calling for help out on the ice of Lake Michigan. Kihlmire and his crew arrived at the shore shortly after 8:00 PM. They could barely make out a person about 200 yards out on the lake. It was a man who had been driving a snowmobile in the snowstorm and had lost his way. He had drifted out onto the lake and fell through a patch of thin ice. Now he clung to the ice as he screamed for help. Hypothermia was setting in, and his strength was failing. Kihlmire had to act quickly.

Kihlmire put on a wet suit, a life jacket, and a special harness attached to a line that other crew members secured on shore. In the icy wind and stinging snow, Kihlmire crawled out on the ice, holding a flashlight in his mouth. His limbs frequently broke through the ice as he crawled. Finally, he reached the nearly unconscious man. Several other Coast Guard personnel had crawled out after Kihlmire, and together they slowly dragged the man toward the

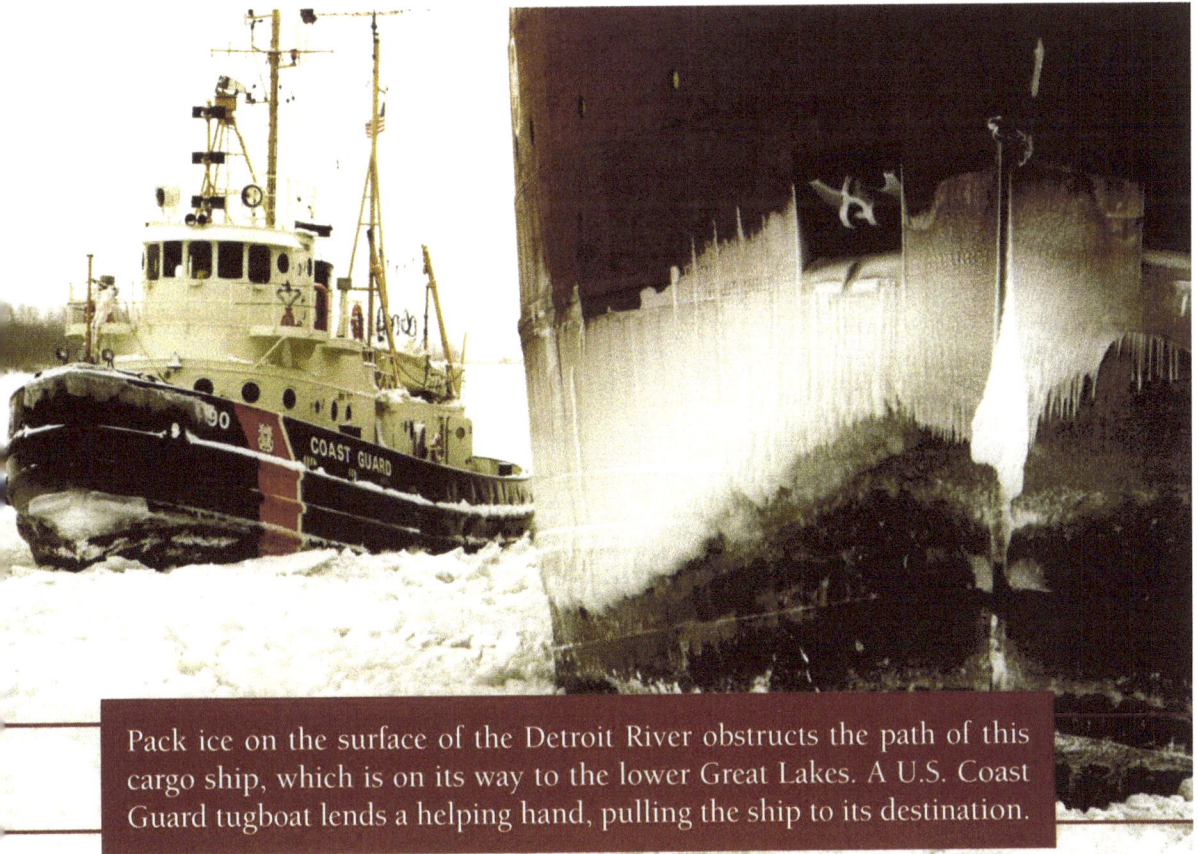

Pack ice on the surface of the Detroit River obstructs the path of this cargo ship, which is on its way to the lower Great Lakes. A U.S. Coast Guard tugboat lends a helping hand, pulling the ship to its destination.

shore. The ice around them kept breaking, and the icy waters nearly dragged them down. They reached thicker ice and worked the victim into a sled that they had brought out to him. Back on shore, they raced the man to a waiting ambulance.

The whole ordeal had taken about fifteen minutes. Thanks to the quick actions of Petty Officer Kihlmire and his crew, the man was saved. Unfortunately, they realized too late that the man's brother had also crashed through the ice. They went back and searched for him, but he was never found.

This story exemplifies the wide range of duties and emotions associated with many search and rescue operations. Kihlmire and his crew rushed back into a perilous situation when they realized that there had been a second man, despite the fact that they knew he probably could not be saved. While Kihlmire and his crew were rewarded for their bravery, a life was lost to the waters that stormy night.

A Perilous Rescue

This true story is based on an article that first appeared in *People* magazine on July 31, 2000.

On October 30, 1991, rescue swimmer David Moore joined his crewmates for a dangerous rescue mission 60 miles (96.6 km) south of Martha's Vineyard, Massachusetts. A massive storm had hit the area, and a small sailboat called the *Satori* was in danger of being destroyed by monstrous waves, some nearly 80 feet (24.4 m) high. At first, the helicopter crew was sent as a precaution, since a Coast Guard cutter, the *Tamaroa*, was on-site to make the rescue. The crew members from the Coast Guard cutter were soon in danger of drowning, and David Moore was forced to jump into action.

Moore dived into the churning waters below the helicopter. He immediately felt lost among the towering waves. It was so bad that Moore needed to go back up to the helicopter to try another dive. The second time he landed closer to the *Satori* and the three members of its panicked crew. He struggled until he had all three safely in the helicopter. Moore then dived back into the turbulent waters a third time to rescue the crew of the *Tamaroa*.

The Coast Guard rescuers were not finished, however. There were other guardspeople in danger. Another Coast Guard helicopter went down just 15 miles (24 km) from where the *Satori* rescue had occurred, leaving its crew to be tossed about by waves 70 to 80 feet (21 to 24 m) tall. The battered crew was miraculously saved by a third helicopter rescue team that had been in the area. The crew of the *Tamaroa* went on to save another boater, despite being rescued themselves just hours before. Tragically, one member of the crew died in the violent storm and was never recovered.

On this day, members of the Coast Guard were called upon to rescue both civilian and Coast Guard personnel. Considering the chaotic weather conditions, it was remarkable that only one person was lost to the storm. This event was related in a 1977 book and a film in 2000, both called *The Perfect Storm*.

CHAPTER 5
How September 11, 2001, Changed the Coast Guard

Immediately after the attack on the World Trade Center, it was obvious to U.S. leaders that security measures would have to change, and that it would take the cooperation of numerous agencies and individuals. How would the Coast Guard and the other branches of the armed forces respond to the tragic events of 9/11? What changes would have to be made in order to ensure the safety of millions of people? Those were questions that had to be considered and answered quickly.

Changes were made, and quickly. As a first line of defense, the Coast Guard was expected to make many of these changes. U.S. ports are very important to the U.S. economy because of the large volume of people, ships, and packages that pass through them every day. In light of this, it is probably obvious that most of the changes the Coast Guard made were related to keeping U.S. ports safe.

In the days following the World Trade Center attack, more than 50 percent of the Coast Guard's budget was used for port security, compared to the 2 percent given to port security before September 11, 2001. As of September 14, 2001, no nonmilitary vessels may come within 100 yards (91.4 m) of U.S. Navy ships unless they first receive permission. To enforce these rules, the Coast Guard patrols the safety zones around navy ships. Other security zones were set up around power plants, marine services, and hazardous freight vessels. The Coast Guard also extended the advance notice a vessel must give before entering a U.S. port from twenty hours to ninety-six hours. This gives the Coast Guard more time to investigate the vessel.

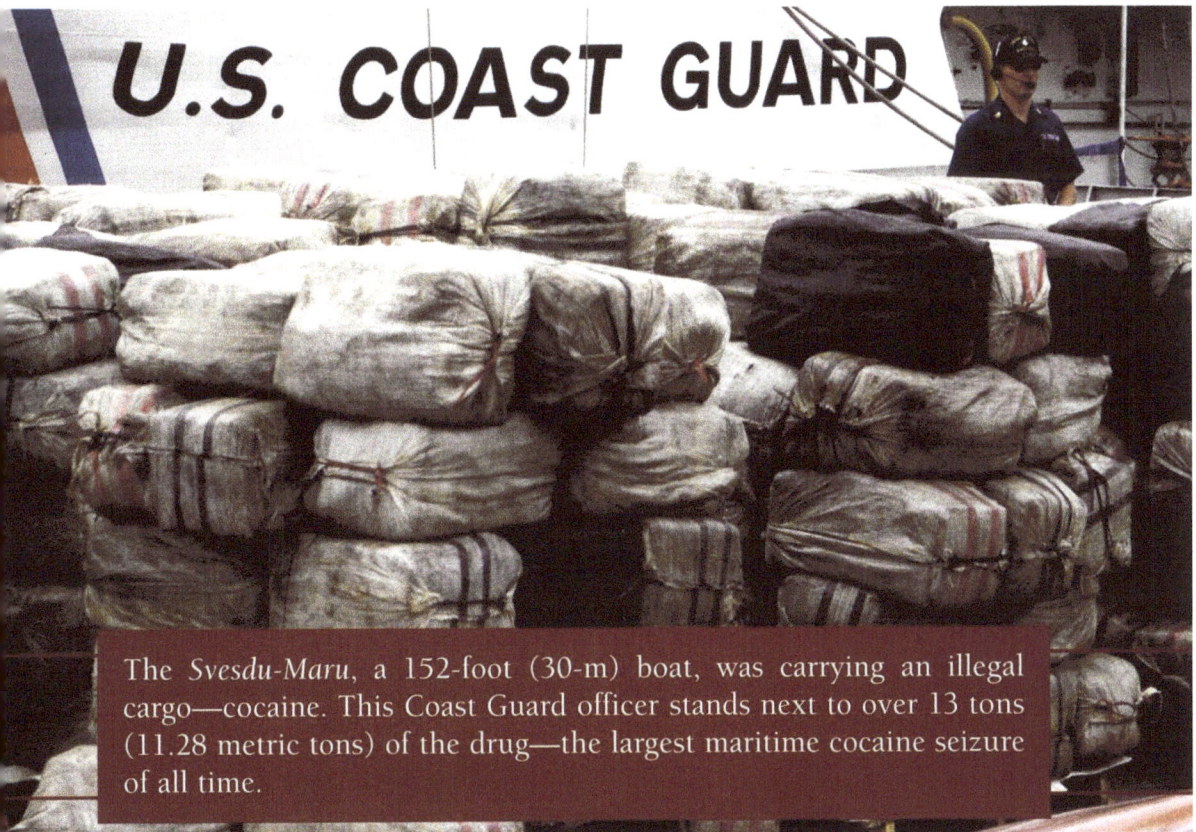

The *Svesdu-Maru*, a 152-foot (30-m) boat, was carrying an illegal cargo—cocaine. This Coast Guard officer stands next to over 13 tons (11.28 metric tons) of the drug—the largest maritime cocaine seizure of all time.

U.S. Coast Guard Core Values

In 1994, the Coast Guard Academy established core values for their officers. These core values have become a very important aspect of training new officers. They have also become guiding principles for all Coast Guard personnel. Since 1998, Coast Guard Academy cadets are evaluated in part according to the three Coast Guard core values. The following is the official Coast Guard report regarding their core values:

Honor: Integrity is our standard. We demonstrate uncompromising ethical conduct and moral behavior in all of our personal actions. We are loyal and accountable to the public trust.

Respect: We value our diverse work force. We treat each other with fairness, dignity, and compassion. We encourage creativity through empowerment. We work as a team.

Devotion to Duty: We are professionals, military and civilian, who seek responsibility, accept accountability, and are committed to the successful achievement of our organizational goals. We exist to serve. We serve with pride.

Several key issues soon came to the forefront as matters that are vital to homeland security. Boating safety was another important issue. Improved boating safety means less time spent on search and rescue missions and more time to protect navy ships and ports. The Coast Guard wanted to improve communication between its divisions, and between itself and federal, state, and local agencies, as well as civilian boaters. The Coast Guard wanted to improve the transportation system so that people could get the most out of the U.S. waterways while providing the most protection; this could include anything from implementing the use of tamper-proof containers for shipping to improving the control of high-priority ships, such as oil tankers and cruise ships. Equipment and vessels needed to be updated.

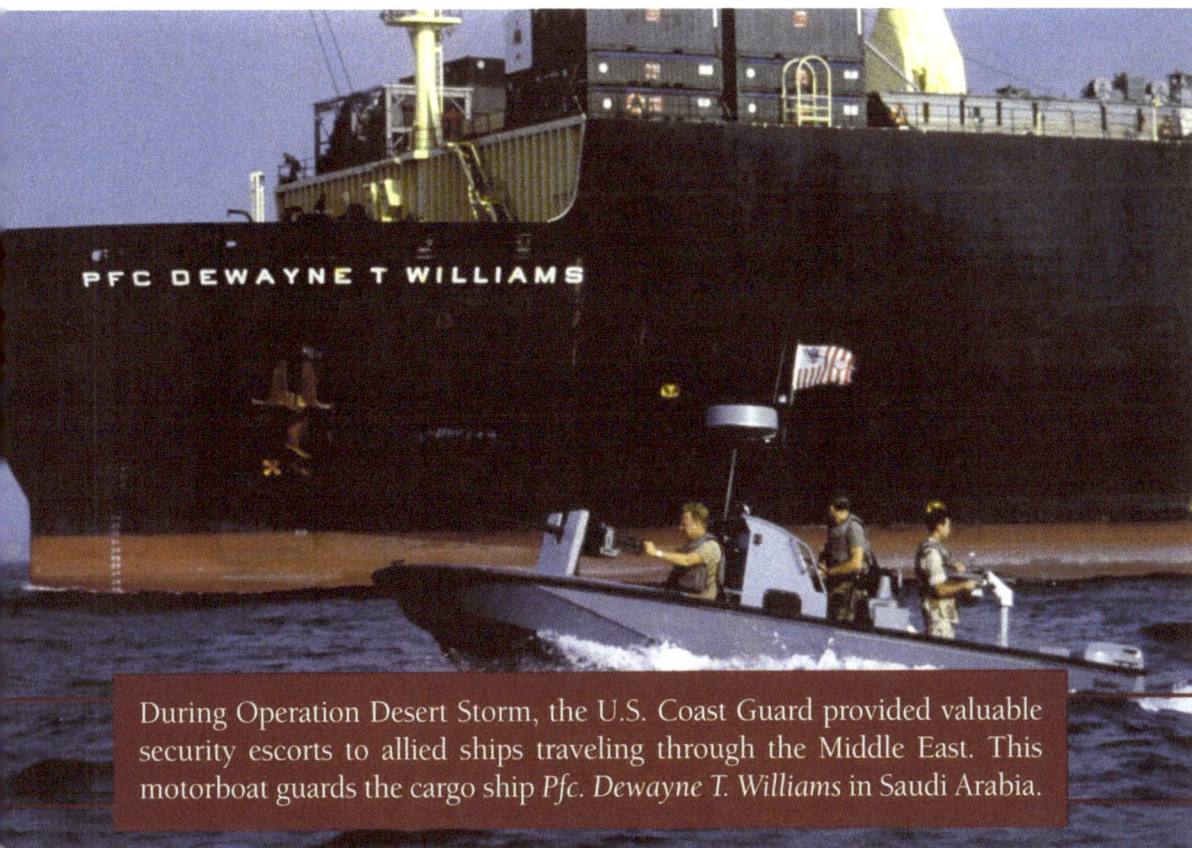

During Operation Desert Storm, the U.S. Coast Guard provided valuable security escorts to allied ships traveling through the Middle East. This motorboat guards the cargo ship *Pfc. Dewayne T. Williams* in Saudi Arabia.

Technology and information systems needed to be modernized. Training needed to be redesigned to ensure that members of the Coast Guard were properly prepared for modern dilemmas. The Coast Guard needed to concentrate on developing the deep-water project to improve their ability to respond to unforeseen dangers. On top of all these changes, the Coast Guard also vowed to stay dedicated to all of their duties, from search and rescue to environmental protection.

Is this a difficult mission? Absolutely, but the Coast Guard is up to it. They have always been responsible for adapting to new dangers and for solving new problems. In the years to come, the Coast Guard will continue to evolve as America's needs arise, and Coast Guard members will always be prepared to risk their lives while protecting American citizens and property. Whether they are called upon to protect ports, to go overseas to assist the U.S. Navy, or to perform vital search and rescue missions close to home, the U.S. Coast Guard will stand by their motto: Semper Paratus—always ready.

GLOSSARY

amphibious Able to function on land or in air and in water.

anthem A song celebrating the greatness of a country or an organization.

beacon A powerful light or horn used to guide vessels near coastal areas.

buoy A floating object anchored in shallow waters that marks a safe path for vessels.

cadet A student at a military school who is training to be an officer.

contraband Goods that are illegal to import, export, and possess.

cutter A small, fast Coast Guard ship designed to "cut" through waves.

hypothermia Dangerously low body temperature.

lightship A ship with a powerful light, used in place of a lighthouse.

maritime Of or relating to the sea.

Mayday An international radio and telephone word used as a distress signal.

navigation The act of planning a course for a ship or an aircraft.

radar The method of detecting distant objects by analyzing radio waves reflected from their surfaces.

recruit A new member of a military force.

smuggle To secretly and unlawfully import or export goods without paying the taxes normally placed on those goods.

standard A flag or banner, especially that of a military force.

tariff A fee or list of fees imposed by a government on imported and exported goods.

terrorism The unlawful use of force or violence to intimidate societies or governments, often for ideological reasons.

vessel A ship, usually larger than a rowboat.

FOR MORE INFORMATION

The American Legion
National Headquarters
Indianapolis Office
700 North Pennsylvania Street
P.O. Box 1055
Indianapolis, IN 46206
(317) 630-1200
Web site: http://www.legion.org

The National Association for Uniformed Services
5535 Hempstead Way
Springfield, VA 22151
(703) 750-1342
Web site: http://www.naus.org

United Armed Forces Association
P.O. Box 20672
Waco, TX 76702
(888) 457-7667
Web site: http://www.uafa.org

Women Officers Professional Association
WOPA
P.O. Box 1621
Arlington, VA 22210
Web site: http://www.wopa.org

Web Sites

Due to the changing nature of Internet links, the Rosen Publishing Group, Inc., has developed an online list of Web sites related to the subject of this book. This site is updated regularly. Please use this link to access the list:

http://www.rosenlinks.com/csro/cgsr/

FOR FURTHER READING

Canney, Donald L. *U.S. Coast Guard and Revenue Cutters, 1790–1935*. Annapolis, MD: Naval Institute Press, 1995.

Department of Defense. *21st Century Complete Guide to the U.S. Coast Guard: Current Events, News, Homeland Security, Immigration, Vessels, Aircraft, Lighthouses, Polar Icebreaking, History, At War, and Safety*. CD-ROM. Progressive Management, 2002.

Johnson, Robert Erwin. *Guardians of the Sea: History of the United States Coast Guard, 1915 to the Present*. Annapolis, MD: Naval Institute Press, 1988.

Larzelere, Alex, and Brent Scowcroft. *The Coast Guard at War: Vietnam, 1965–1975*. Annapolis, MD: Naval Institute Press, 1997.

Noble, Dennis L. *That Others Might Live: The U.S. Life-Saving Service, 1878–1915*. Annapolis, MD: Naval Institute Press, 1994.

Shanks, Ralph C., Wick York, and Lisa Woo Shanks, ed. *The U.S. Life-Saving Service: Heroes, Rescues, and Architecture of the Early Coast Guard*. Petaluma, CA: Costāno Books, 1996.

Stonehouse, Frederick. *Lighthouse Keepers & Coast Guard Cutters: Heroic Lighthouse Keepers and the Coast Guard Cutters Named After Them*. Gwinn, MI: Avery Color Studios, Inc., 2000.

BIBLIOGRAPHY

American Maritime Congress. "After 9/11: Maritime News
    Following the Tragedy." Retrieved March 25, 2002
    (http://www.us-flag.org/af911marnewf.html).

Carney, James C. "U.S. Coast Guard: The 'Forgotten' Military."
    2001. Retrieved May 15, 2002 (http://www.jacksjoint.com/
    the_forgotten_military.htm).

Ferrell, Nancy Warren. *The U.S. Coast Guard*. Minneapolis,
    MN: Lerner Publications, 1989.

Grunts.net. "United States Coast Guard: Search and Rescue."
    Retrieved May 16, 2002 (http://www.grunts.net/
    uscg/sar.html).

Hamilton, Robert A. TheDay.com. "New Methods of Protecting
    Ports Needed: Coast Guard Expert Says Terrorist Targets Are
    Many." February 7, 2002. Retrieved March 25, 2002
    (http://www.theday.com/news/sp-report3.asp?NewsUID=
    0A2822B4-9D6C-4551-8B65-6EB11C4BA3D4&rec=9).

Herbert, James W. "U.S. Coast Guard Ranks." 1996. Retrieved May 16, 2002 (http://continuouswave.com/boats/bristolBay/rank.html).

Korb, Lawrence J. Council on Foreign Relations. "Meeting Summary. Homeland Security: A Coast Guard Perspective." 2001. Retrieved June 4, 2002 (http://www.cfr.org/public/resource.cgi?pub!4355).

Krietemeyer, Captain George E. *The Coast Guardsman's Manual*. Annapolis, MD: Naval Institute Press, 2000.

Noble, Dennis L. "A Legacy: The United States Life-Saving Service." November 2001. Retrieved May 15, 2002 (http://www.uscg.mil/hq/g-cp/history/h_USLSS.html).

Noble, Dennis L. *Lifeboat Sailors*. Washington, DC: Brassey's, 2000.

Scheina, Robert. "The Coast Guard at War." January 1999. Retrieved May 15, 2002 (http://www.uscg.mil/hq/g-cp/history/h_Cgatwar.html).

Scheina, Robert. "U.S Coast Guard: A Historical Overview." January 1999. Retrieved May 15, 2002 (http://www.uscg.mil/hq/g-cp/history/h_USCGhistory.html).

Snyder, John. "Ferries to the Rescue After World Trade Center Terror Attack." October 2001. Retrieved June 4, 2002 (http://www.marinelog.com/DOCS/PRINT/mmiocfer1.html).

TheDay.com. "Securing the Border." February 16, 2002. Retrieved March 25, 2002 (http://www.theday.com/news/

sp-report3.asp?NewsUID=B888C9E4-B087-426D-9206-CCA06078C812&rec=9).

United States Coast Guard. "A Brief History of the Coast Guard Reserve." June 1995. Retrieved May 15, 2002 (http://www.uscg.mil/hq/reserve/reshist.htm).

United States Coast Guard. "The Coast Guard & Homeland Security." January 2002. Retrieved May 15, 2002 (http://www.uscg.mil/hq/g-cp/history/Homeland_Security.html).

United States Coast Guard. "Coast Guard Rescue Swimmers." January 2002. Retrieved May 15, 2002 (http://www.uscg.mil/hq/g-cp/history/Rescue_Swimmer_History.html).

United States Coast Guard. "Deepwater Roles & Missions." Retrieved May 29, 2002 (http://www.uscg.mil/hq/g-a/Deepwater/MISSIONS/Missions%20Assets%20History.htm).

United States Coast Guard. "Enlisted Rating Guide." January 2001. Retrieved May 15, 2002 (http://www.uscg.mil/overview/InsigniaCombined14.jpg).

United States Coast Guard. "The Essence of the Coast Guard: America's Maritime Guardians." Retrieved May 15, 2002 (http://www.uscg.mil/overview/essence_of_the_coast_guard.htm).

United States Coast Guard. "Homeland Security." March 2002. Retrieved May 29, 2002 (http://www.uscg.mil/hq/g-a/Deepwater/MISSIONS/threats.htm).

United States Coast Guard. "International Ice Patrol History." Retrieved May 29, 2002 (http://www.uscg.mil/lantarea/iip/iiphist.html).

United States Coast Guard. "International Ice Patrol Mission." Retrieved May 29, 2002 (http://www.uscg.mil/lantarea/iip/iipmis.html).

United States Coast Guard. "New Rules to Fight Terrorism Announced." May 28, 2002. Retrieved May 29, 2002 (http://www.uscg.mil/d5/news/2002/r052_02.html).

United States Coast Guard. "Recreational Boating Safety." Retrieved May 30, 2002 (http://www.uscg.mil/overview/issue%20rbs.htm).

United States Coast Guard. "Sinbad, USCG (Ret.): K9C (Chief Petty Officer, Dog)." October 2001. Retrieved March 15, 2002 (http://www.uscg.mil/hq/g%2Dcp/history/faqs/sinbad.html).

United States Coast Guard. "U.S. Coast Guard Core Values." Retrieved May 16, 2002 (http://www.uscg.mil/hq/g%2Dw/g%2Dwt/g%2Dwtl/values.htm).

United States Coast Guard: Office of Boating Safety. "Tips for Preventing Boating Injuries and Fatalities." Retrieved May 30, 2002 (http://www.uscgboating.org/saf/saf_yrdeathgraph.asp).

United States Coast Guard Academy. "Academy History and General Information." July 1998. Retrieved May 15, 2002 (http://www.cga.edu/history.html).

The Wheelhouse Report. "The Coast Guard Responds to the Terrorist Attacks." Retrieved June 4, 2002 (http://www.wheelhousereport.org/to/cg/cgresp.html).

INDEX

A

Alaska, 17, 33
American Revolution, 10–11

B

bachelor's degree, 24
basic training, 23
beacons, 14, 33
boating safety and inspection, 17–20,
    25–27, 30–32, 48
buoys, 5, 13–15, 33
Bureau of Navigation, 21

C

cadets, 24–25
Caribbean Sea, 16
Coast Guard
    anthem, 8–9
    Academy, 24–25
    Auxiliary, 25–27, 31
    benefits, 23, 25
    boot camp for, 22–23
    history of, 10–21
    law enforcement duties of, 12–13
    peacetime duties of, 29–34
    professions, 22
    ranks of, 26
    Reserves, 25, 27
    response to terrorist attacks of
        September 11, 2001, 4–8,
        46–50
    salary, 23
    vessels of, 37, 39
    wartime duties of, 28–29
    women in, 27–28
Coast Guard Academy, 24–25
Coast Guard Auxiliary, 25–27, 31
Coast Guard Reserves, 25, 27
Coasties, 15
Continental navy, 15
contraband, 13, 28
cutter, 6, 9, 12, 22, 28, 33, 36–37, 45

D

deepwater program, 21

E

educational experience, 24
Eighteenth Amendment, 13
ensign, 25

F

Federal Boat Safety Act, 30
fishery laws, 32
Fulton, Robert, 17

G

global positioning system, 34, 38

H

Hamilton, Alexander, 11–12
helicopters, 21, 37–38, 40–41, 45
homeland security, 13, 16, 29, 48
hypothermia, 41, 43

I

ice breakers, 33, 37
illegal drugs, 13
International Ice Observation and Ice
    Patrol Service, 33
international ice patrol and ice breaking,
    32–33

K

Kihlmire, Dennis L., 42–44

L

lifeboats, 35, 39
Lifeboat Sailors, 42
Life-Saving Service, 20, 21, 36
lighthouses, 13, 14, 15, 33
lightships, 13, 15
LORAN (Long Range Aid to Navigation),
    27, 34, 38

M

Marine Electric, 41
marine wildlife, 6, 32
maritime safety, 15, 20
Moore, David, 44–45
Motorboat Act, 20

N

navigation, 15
navigational aids, 13, 33–34
Nazi submarines, 29

O

oil spills, 17, 32

P

Perfect Storm, The, 45
pirates, 12, 28
pollution, 17, 27–28, 32
ports, 46
Prohibition, 13

R

radar, 37–38
rapid response cleanup team, 32
recreational boaters, 30
recruits, 22–23
rescue swimmers, 37, 40–41
reservists, 6, 9, 25, 27
RMS *Titanic*, 32

S

Satori, 44–45
search and rescue, 20–21, 34,
    35–41
Semper Paratus, 8–9, 50
Sinbad (Coast Guard dog), 18
slave trade, 12
smugglers, 6, 11–12, 13
Steamboat Inspection Act, 19
Steamboat Inspection Service, 17,
    19, 21

T

Tamaroa, 45
tariff, 11, 28
timber reserve, 17

U

U.S. Constitution, 13
U.S. Navy, 15, 28, 29, 50

V

Van Boskerck, Francis Saltus, 8–9
Vessel Safety Check program, 31
volunteers, 25

W

War of 1812, 16
Washington, George, 11
Wilson, Woodrow, 33
World Trade Center, 4, 46
World War II, 16, 25, 27, 29, 34

About the Author

Greg Roza is a children's book editor and a freelance author living in upstate New York with his wife, Abigail, and their daughter, Autumn.

Photo Credits

Cover, pp. 5, 19, 40, 47, 49 © Corbis; p. 1 © Brandon Brewer/AP/Wide World Photos; p. 7 © Scott Carr/AP/Wide World Photos; p. 11 © U.S. Coast Guard; p. 14 © Chris Rainier/Corbis; p. 24 © Todd Gipstein/Corbis; p. 31 © AP/ Wide World Photos; p. 36 © Jeremiah Coughlan/AP/Wide World Photos; p. 39 © Bojan Breceli/Corbis; p. 43 © James L. Amos/Corbis.

Editor

Annie Sommers

Designer

Nelson Sá

www.ingramcontent.com/pod-product-compliance
Lightning Source LLC
Chambersburg PA
CBHW061136030426
42334CB00003B/62

3. Regularly disseminate our own compelling narrative as well as counter-narratives to adversarial narratives

As noted at the outset, large-scale influence campaigns are by default, Narrative Warfare. These weaponized narratives along with all supporting efforts in such a campaign are oriented towards the meaning set out in an adversary's narrative. Such meaning loosely or sometimes specifically identifies an adversary's intended objectives of their campaign. While in military planning parlance, objectives, courses of action, restraints/constraints etc. have specific meaning, it is unhelpful to adhere to the very narrow definitions of military planning. Most military planning is linear in nature. Influence is dimensional in nature. Using one to achieve results in the other is the planning equivalent of attempting to "put a square peg in a round hole". The bottom line to this is that planning matters. The right type of planning matters more... and executing the right plan with the required resources matters the most.

Remember, narrative is about identity and meaning. Narratives, well-constructed deliver meaning to a series of issues and events so that audiences don't sort the meaning out on their own. Merely disseminating sterile press releases (PRs) will not accomplish furthering our agenda since they typically only provide facts. PRs. though are excellent supporting messages to an over-arching narrative if well-constructed to deliver meaning, rather than sterile facts. Meaning is critical in that both Allies and adversaries are often confused by our disparate actions and words simply because we have not bothered to explain the meaning of our words and actions. Both Allies and adversaries need to clearly understand what we're doing and why.

The inherent risk of only messaging isolated and unrelated facts without attaching meaning is that the adversary could attach their meaning to the same facts. This means you've allowed the adversary, in this case Russia, to control the meaning of events, factual or otherwise.

In terms of the role of narrative, offensive and defensive, it is important to understand some basic differences in narrative terminology. The following three explanations matter the most in a strategy:

Weaponized Narrative

The term "Weaponized Narrative" (WN) has come into relative prominence in the wake of Russian efforts against the West. WN is a piece of an overarching narrative strategy. WN, a specialized type of narrative is designed to fill the cognitive space that specifically targets the vulnerabilities of an adversary by establishing meaning, not fact which triggers behavior, sustains the initiative, and crowds out competing narratives. Once established, simply countering such a narrative is very difficult without a compelling narrative of your own.

In the case of Russian meddling in the US and other Western nations, the Russian narrative or as discussed later, "family of narratives" were designed to trigger predictable behavior in the identity of separate and opposing elements of Western society as well as sell Russian legitimacy for their acts of aggression in places like Ukraine and Syria.

Weaponized narrative is powerful because it targets predictable behavior by way of emotional responses, most often fear. This subset of WN can often be described as "conflict narrative."

Operational or Comprehensive Narrative Strategy

Operational Narrative or a comprehensive narrative strategy is a complete package of both offensive and defensive narratives coordinated to both degrade adversarial audiences and to build resilience within friendly audiences. When thinking about a complete narrative strategy, a good analogy is a sport such as football that includes both offensive and defensive strategy and more importantly, a game plan which encompasses both.

As with any sporting event, the team must play both offensive and defense, execute a game plan and play at a superior level if your team is to win. Not employing any of these elements most often results in a loss for your team. In the case of Russia vs. many Western nations, this has been and still is to some extent the case. Simply put, Russia is deploying a powerful offensive or weaponized narrative strategy with impunity and largely unopposed. Their vulnerability though is that they are not playing much defense except by insulating their populace from a Western narrative by restrictive measures such as isolating friendly audiences and by technical methods such as CYBER.

Family of Narratives

FoN, or Family of Narratives is a far more complex but requisite construct. I will try and simplify as much as possible and again use Russian information warfare as the example.

Russia does not only deploy a WN that says they are good, honest, and strong while contrasting the West as weak, divided and a threat to themselves and others. To sell this idea they use a great many sub-narratives designed to highlight divisive issues in Western society.

Divisive Issues Highlighted in Russian Sub Narratives

1. Migration
2. Nationalism
3. Racial issues
4. Economic disparity
5. Hypocrisy
6. Russian strength and legitimate rights such as:
7. Russian involvement in Ukraine is based on a distorted right to assert protection of Russians at risk from a corrupt Ukrainian government.
8. Russia is the good and loyal friend of Syria wishing only to destroy terrorists and support the rightful government,
9. NATO is encroaching on Russia's western border and is a threat.

These sub-narratives are what are best described as a **family of narratives**. All speak to different identities of different audiences, all portray meaning, not truth and all are delivered in a form most suited to triggering predictable behavior in each audience. All support their overarching narrative and attendant themes and most importantly, each "family member" supports the family narrative as a whole.

With the above understanding, US/Allied influence strategy must employ a comprehensive narrative strategy as described in the portions; Operational Narrative and FoN or Family of Narratives.

How we accomplish this then becomes the question. This question also identifies one of our US most critical vulnerabilities. The US, since the demise of the USIA (US Information Agency) in the mid-1990s and the side-lining of Strategic Communications in 2012 at the Pentagon, has lost critical players responsible for strategic narrative. The Pentagon and Office of the Secretary of Defense have largely tried to make up for these losses by shifting to a Public Affairs (PA) approach and dependence on the US Department of State (DoS). Neither is currently capable of handling the delicacy nor volume of the task.

Asking PA and DoS alone to manage the strategic narrative task is the military equivalent of telling a political candidate to manage dissemination of their platform and communications by a couple of PAOs and a handful of highly placed friends and without the benefit of media, messaging and related actions under the control of a campaign manager. To make matters worse within the US, most IO related entities self-victimize by way of sibling rivalry over budgets, roles and tasking authority.

Narrative dissemination must be controlled by a central USG coordinating authority that has much the same command and control (C2) as a

31

media service managing a significant political campaign or a marketing firm with global customers. The current architecture of the USG is deficient in nearly every possible way to achieve operational narrative dominance. As that a full-scale narrative strategy must be integrated across strategic, operational and tactical levels simultaneously and responsively, the FoN (family of narratives) concept is nearly impossible without a centralized C2 mechanism.

An aspect of narrative warfare frequently forgotten is that it requires its own unique type of intelligence collection and analysis. Narrative identity analysis (NIA) is not synonymous with target audience analysis (TAA). Typical TAA is centered essentially on demographics/ preferences. Narrative identity analysis is centered on literally, the identity of the audience. Sentiment analysis employed by some marketers, is closer but still not focused on "who the audience" truly is and identifies as. Understanding how to trigger specific identity is precisely the point of influence.

Recommendations

1. Create, staff, and authorize tasking authority to a single USG entity charged with developing, disseminating and assessing strategic communications to include narratives and supporting messaging:

2. This single entity would be civilian lead with a board comprised of senior leaders from DoD, DoS and all other relevant entities including the IC (Intelligence Community)

3. Create a comprehensive narrative strategy that includes a FoNs (family of narratives) that speak to multiple and disparate audiences, friendly and adversarial. Base all narratives on the core principles/ science of narrative: 1. Narrative identity 2. Meaning, not fact 3. Structure/form.

4. Designate a core analysis community of IC professionals that can:

5. track, analyze and assess dissemination of narratives.

6. Identify unique audiences and based on narrative principles undertake NIA (narrative identity analysis).

7. Create a digital TF (task force) with innovative and current technology that collects, analyzes and assesses dissemination of narratives friendly and adversarial.

8. Create a sub-component that synchronizes a US narrative strategy with friendly nations and non-state entities.

9. Ensure that a comprehensive approach to messaging can be achieved to accommodate long and short term (responsive) messaging requirements.

10. Message by all available and appropriate means and message in support of our narrative strategy

Routine and regular messaging in support of the meaning contained in the narrative strategy means that you are managing and controlling the conversation. This is dominance in military-speak. Much like an awkward and disjointed conversation in a social setting, dead-air loses the attention of the audience. When attention and credibility are lost, adversarial messaging can fill the void and change the subject or meaning surrounding events and issues. This does not mean to so overwhelm an audience with nuisance "chatter" but to keep their interest with relevant and culturally nuanced information.

Think of messaging as conversational. We all know people who talk at us with little to say and whom we avoid or "tune-out". We also all know people who we can listen to for extended periods of time because they have information and ideas worthy of our attention. The bottom line is that we must be worthy of holding an audience's attention by being credible and talking with rather than talking at them. Sustained messaging across the spectrum of strategic, operational and tactical (local) requires infrastructure and C2 (Command and Control) capable of managing information flow. I will return to this critical issue in depth, later in this article.

A comprehensive communication strategy which can hold the attention of an audience and exert predictable influence includes messaging which supports and is woven into a narrative strategy. A glaring inadequacy of USG/DoD messaging is the doctrinal addiction the old adage of "themes and messages". Themes and messages as an effective, self-contained communication strategy are a false premise. While the themes and messages are important, they are sub-components of narrative. Themes are the storyline of narrative which give it meaning. Messages merely reinforce those themes. Think of themes and messages as a body walking with legs and arms flailing but headless. This is themes and messages without narrative. Narrative is the missing head that tells the arms and legs where they're going and explains why.

Every action taken in support of USG intentions is a messaging opportunity, good or bad. Remember, narrative is about identity and co-creating identity between narrator and audience. Even messaging around a difficult or negative issue is an opportunity to further the bond between narrator and audience. For example, the issue of collateral damage in Afghanistan by US or NATO forces was at one time so critical that such an event would shut-down operations until the matter could be resolved. Becoming proactive, controlling the narrative with honest and immediate reporting reversed this dynamic nearly 100% of the time. Actions must be taken with narrative and messaging support considered.

Another gross inadequacy of messaging is that the USG, specifically DoD is narrowly focused on specific capabilities or in civilian terms tools, when it comes to influence operations. Only a couple of these tools are considered messengers. This could hardly be further from the most effective messaging architecture. As I learned from my trade as an IO (Information Operations) practitioner, early on that anyone, any entity or any action impacting my target audience was a messaging opportunity. It is not only the USG or the US military that encounters audiences important to what Russia is doing. Nearly every agency within the USG, private companies, NGOs, private citizens ; all are in contact with relevant target audiences. Every single one can and should be considered a part of the influence puzzle. Russia and other adversaries understand this very well and employ this strategy against us with startlingly effective results. Ignoring this aspect by antiquated adherence to doctrine is precisely analogous to fighting with one or both hands tied behind our back.

No focus on messaging would be complete without calling out one of our most glaring discrepancies, lack of cultural nuance in messaging. For a nation of immigrants our messaging is painfully devoid of cultural nuance. This is not just in regard to the message per se but also in regard to the delivery methods and messengers. Again, in regard to narrative, the issue of identity is key. Cultural nuance that addresses specific identity is the bond created between the narrator or the messenger and the audience.

The bottom line to a messaging strategy is that analysis, integration, and command & control that are both visionary and responsive are critical. Russian influence operations operate with this axiom. Russian strategy regarding influence shares a great deal in common with ours. The primary difference though is that Russia employs, assesses, and recalibrates for more effectiveness. Yes, there is much handwringing within USG/ DoD circles regarding oversight, authorities, and integration but handwringing, think-tanking and failure to execute across the spectrum of the USG still hobble US efforts.

Actions must demonstrate a firm resistance to aggression

As previously noted, Russia is much the schoolyard bully, albeit far more dangerous. Firm, unrelenting and well explained deterrence, including painful consequences are currently the best option for slowing Russian aggression. Strong deterrence only buys what the US military calls white space. It would allow us to catch our breath, form/execute a strategy that includes the 5 recommended courses of action in this article. There are many forms of deterrence, and they all need to be explored in support of delivering the most balanced and proportionate response. The recent sanctions on nineteen Russian individuals and entities are valuable. CYBER deterrence is valuable in that it demonstrates to Russia that living by the sword means dying by the sword. Again, the paradigm of proportionality is key. We're not looking for war but stability that is sustainable and secure. This concept is very much the same as Cold War MAD (mutually assured destruction) concepts.

Regardless of the type of deterrence employed, it could hardly be more important that both Russia and our Allies clearly understand our intent, resolve and depth in deploying deterrence. Narrative is the only means by which effective communication of who we are and what we intend can be delivered.

Every theme and message regarding deterrence must be tied to our overarching narrative about who we are and what we will stand for or not. Every PR regarding our actions, every action taken and every ramification of our actions regarding our Allies must be explained by way of narrative principles so that we are not misunderstood and so that we do not edge closer to open conflict. Deterrence, above all else is a message and must be delivered with all the nuance and sensitivity of any effective messaging.

All historians well remember the lessons of "The Guns of August", when actions and messages caused catastrophic miscalculation and all-out war in 1914. Nuanced strategy, narrative-centric messaging, and carefully proportionate actions (also messages) reinforce order, stability and mitigate the most dangerous aspects of brinkmanship.

Deterrence, like all components of influence operations requires exacting and detailed analysis which demands innovation in what we collect and how we analyze and synthesize collection. Human terrain analysis, including in the digital realm currently is not a specialty of US and many Western Allies. All influence requires "knowing your adversary". Narrative identity analysis as an example, requires psycho-cultural analysis which is far more exacting than what can be provided in scale by our current intelligence disciplines. In short, what works for deterrence in regard to one target group or state, very likely will not be as effective in other groups. Deterrence tailored to a specific target group is the key to proportionate and effective deterrence.

Recommendations:

1. Integrate all action & deterrence with coordinating messaging along with the recommended messaging entity in order to shape cognitive environments and fully exploit all deterrent actions as they occur.

2. Though it is implied, it is critical to understand that deterrence measures taken in the CYBER realm must be integrated with all other messaging elements rather than operating in isolation from all other influence efforts.

3. Pre and post activity assess the effects of deterrence measures as to risk along with pre-planned contingency actions.

4. Pre and post coordinate with affected state and non-state partners likely to be impacted by such measures.

Putting it all together

As with any strategy, it is not the individual elements alone that matter. While each of the five components of this recommendation are critical to the whole strategy, they are not stand-alone. None will achieve significant results in the absence of employing all five to their fullest effect, choreographed within the parameters of overall strategy.

To achieve the most positive results these five components must be managed by a single entity with tasking authority over the dozens of entities within the USG that hold sway over the relevant pieces. This will mean that those myriad elements give up some control over their assets to contribute to the whole. In our current national security architecture, this is asking a great deal, mostly due to budget issues in which each element fears co-mingling their budgets. Overcoming this and related hurdles will require firm and visionary leadership by the senior leaders of all these agencies, entities, and programs. This also by default will require the IC to break down the institutional barriers of cooperation long seen as prohibitive. Again, if leadership wants to achieve greater results, they will need to force the requisite evolution.

During the Cold War, the US managed the C2 of such activity largely by way of the now defunct USIA (US Information Agency). We disbanded this agency in the late 1990s and are now paying the price. Also, OSD/DoD in the 2011/ 2012 timeframe did away with Strategic Communications. What has been left in their place is a hodgepodge of informal and ineffective collaboration which is more personality dependent than a well-oiled and tuned machine of influence. IO (Information Operations) in theory should coordinate such activities for DoD but for reasons too many to articulate, they here have failed miserably. To be blunt, US leadership responsible for influence activities can no longer afford to merely tinker with the antiquated machinery of influence but immediately undertake radical surgery to rid ourselves of the cancer of bureaucratic protectionism afflicting the US national security community.

As noted under the topic of resiliency, this must become a high priority which underlies much of the other 4 components of the strategy. This is a generational problem at best. As with all long roads, the first step is the hardest. The advantage though is that it is ultimately, the least resource intensive by comparison. Leadership that empowers creative thinking within their organizations to insist on factual, in-context information is critical.

Also, their "lead by example" requirement sets the tone for their organizations. In a hyper political information environment, this may be difficult but should leaders of opposing political persuasions demonstrate courage, it is achievable.

With a hardened information target audience an immediate improvement can be realized. CYBER has a big role in supporting resiliency. Technology which identifies content, outlets, and automated SM, while simultaneously neutralizing divisive content takes the pressure off of audiences all too ready to retreat into their ideological corners.

Offensive CYBER also can and must simultaneously demonstrate through deterrent actions that continued efforts to divide and target US & Allied audiences and infrastructure will not be tolerated. Defensive CYBER can contribute greatly to protecting the data of individuals and organizations which further reduces the hypersensitivity within targeted audiences. Many of the tools exist and must be employed with far fewer prohibitive hand-wringing sessions from those in charge of such tools.

Messaging, messaging and more messaging which is synchronized by a single entity could hardly be more important. For a nation with one of the most capable communication and media communities in existence, we fail miserably short when communicating with the rest of the world in support of our intentions. Like everything within the US government, messaging has become so disjointed, bureaucratic and stove-piped as to be nearly ineffective. One of our most glaring shortcomings is that in a nearly instantaneous information environment, we have a miniscule fraction of the capability to message in a timely fashion. This could hardly be truer than in military environments and especially in regard to coordinating with the rest of the USG. Again, this is a simple fix when applying common-sense supported by visionary leadership, but in our current architecture nearly unachievable for the previously discussed reasons.

Finally, and coming full circle to the beginning point regarding "narrative warfare", we have zero narrative strategy. Virtually every one of the five components of this strategy are based on our intent as a nation. Without communicating who we are, what is the meaning of our actions (or not) in a form that relates our identity to that of our audiences, we will continue to fail. To punctuate this point, I cannot count the times that in conversations with friend and foe alike I have been asked, why is the US doing this or that? What do your actions and messages mean? If we cannot answer these basic questions, we have allowed our adversaries to control the narrative of our actions. Currently, Russia dominates the meaning of US and Allied actions with a "the West is threatening mother Russia and we are merely protecting ourselves with the resources available" narrative. Rebutting this requires that we dominate the narrative space and as we all can see; sporadic and random press releases of rebuttal simply won't do.

So, here's the bottom line: Let's tell our story so that everyone understands it. Let's protect ourselves from adversarial stories and related content. Let's clearly demonstrate to our adversaries that there is a price to pay for their aggression and ultimately, let's make our story worthy of all audiences.

Summary

The simplest reason that there are only five recommended courses of action discussed in this paper is that we are currently in crisis mode. In short, we must act and soon. By all estimations, the ability to develop, resource and staff a competent influence organization is prohibitive in a short period of time. Implementing the basic five-pronged approach with available/re-tasked resources, though daunting in scope and as described in this paper, is still pragmatically streamlined in comparison. The bottom line is that in order to adopt any strategy, short or grand in scale, we must break from decades old national doctrine. Yes, old habits are hard to break... but not impossible.

The take-a-way lesson to this entire discussion regarding an influence strategy for Russia is that in order for any of these recommendations to become effective, we must have an entity which can strategize, coordinate and execute influence. We can no longer afford to hope for successful long-term collaboration without leadership, training, resources, legal authorities and divorcing ourselves from the plodding, protectionist bureaucracy which currently satiates the USG national security community. The latest US DoD budget of $700 plus billion dollars including a windfall of $61 billion in additional funds shows that influence has been nearly ignored. When every reasonable and credible defense analyst is declaring that conflict beneath the threshold of all-out war is the new norm, the logic for focusing on bombers, ships and tanks is fatally flawed. Common sense dictates that prioritized planning for threats needs to be based on analysis, not the bottom line of big defense contractors. Our current analysis says clearly, that conflicts are now influence-centric and so by default, common sense requires prioritizing resources in a manner that meets the needs of regaining influence dominance.

As noted in the aforementioned sports analogy of football; we cannot compete without all the players, a playbook, training, support staff, recruiting, innovation and the requisite resources for everyone from the water-boy to the coach. The coach also must have control of the entire apparatus who can make the necessary adjustments as the game evolves. Anything less results in regular and routine failure. This failure is precisely what we now are experiencing.

Finally, a reminder that "Influence done well is a complex and intricate choreography of actions, words and related activities". Just the bare minimum requirements and related discussion have fully filled the preceding pages, with far too much still unsaid. I have little doubt that there will be firm and detailed resistance from many of the communities now charged with the tasks of influence and I welcome it. Intense and detailed professional discussion is required for problem solving. Action, resulting from those discussions is even more important. If this paper encourages and prompts such action, even in the face of criticism, it will have been worth the effort. A reminder to those that would challenge me; as with the quote at the very beginning of this paper; *don't just complain, present solutions.*

2
The US 2020 Presidential Election

Shortly after the first essay in this book was first published, in mid-2018, the Knight Foundation published the first open source, large scale analysis of Twitter's role in the Russian influence campaign during the 2016 Presidential election period. The 61 pages of meticulous research provided some dramatic insights into a new weapon of warfare, narrative warfare to be precise.

Many of the 13 primary points made during the Knight Foundations' research were new to the US at the time. As of this writing, much of the threat aspects addressed in the study, still are significantly vulnerable. The US national security community has either been unwilling or unable to address all aspects, sometimes for good reasons, often not. There are some technical improvements, CYBER related surveillance, and tools not available in 2016 which are very good at filling some of our security gaps. What's left unaddressed will fall mainly on the shoulders of informed and committed US patriots to defend. The bad news is that the USG is not handling everything. The good news is that with some mentorship, leadership and training, US citizens can fill many of the remaining gaps.

Homeland Security Today Magazine: *Anatomy of Narrative Warfare and Social Media Ops Since the Last Presidential election*

Published October 30, 2018

In the months since the 2016 Presidential election there have been countless words written regarding influence, misinformation, the ever-present "fake news," etc. One of the most fertile social media platforms for this type of activity was and still is Twitter, which is still the "Wild West" of social media.

The Knight Foundation recently published one of the largest studies and analysis that is publicly available to date regarding "fake news" on Twitter. The 61-page study, meticulously cited, is worth a careful read and saved for future reference. "Fake news" is just one aspect of malign influence campaigns whether this influence originates from foreign adversaries or unscrupulous, witting and unwitting domestic players. Malign influence is a threat to U.S. national security and, by extension, to our allies as well.

What follows is some basic perspective about where and how this type of analysis fits into the national security landscape. Of note, I will say that the topic is complex, to say the least. A great deal of scrutiny regarding the findings of this excellent piece of work is not only due but required for national security professionals in addition to well-informed citizens from other walks of life. Protecting the nation from malign influence is not exclusively the role of professionals but also the responsibility of citizenship. In terms of protecting the homeland, this study does, though, provide some of the best large-scale insights for national security professionals to date.

As you read this article, it would be helpful to also have reviewed the study, especially the executive summary that highlights 13 primary findings.

Additionally, I will also state categorically that the role of mis- or disinformation in social media is made far more effective because it plays on the principles of and directly supports malign narratives.

For the record, influence as a whole and the role of narrative in influence is my profession, honed over a career in the U.S. Army and now privately as the VP of Narrative Strategies, a U.S.-based think-and-do tank that focuses on the role of influence in national security matters.

Narrative is as natural to human beings as breathing. We are meaning-seeking animals, and our primary means of meaning-making is narrative. Narrative is the way we create, transmit and, in some cases, negotiate meaning. Without narrative, life would be experienced as an unconnected and overwhelming series of random events. We organize, prioritize, and order our experiences through narratives that we usually inherit. What's more, we understand not only the world around us but also ourselves through the narratives we live by; our personal narratives inform our personal identities, our tribal/familial narratives inform our tribal/familial identities, and our national narratives inform our national identity.

"Life stories do not simply reflect personality. They are personality, or more accurately, they are important parts of personality, along with other parts, like dispositional traits, goals, and values," writes Dan McAdams, a professor of psychology at Northwestern University, along with Erika Manczak in a chapter for the *APA Handbook of Personality and Social Psychology.*

13 Primary Findings from the Knight Foundation Study

1. This study is one of the largest analyses to date on how fake news spread on Twitter both during and after the 2016 Presidential election campaign.

2. Much fake news and disinformation is still being spread on Twitter.

3. Just a few fake and conspiracy outlets dominated during the Presidential election – and nearly all of them continue to dominate today.

4. Our methods find much more fake and conspiracy news activity on Twitter than several recent high-profile studies – though fake news still receives significantly fewer links than mainstream media sources.

5. Most accounts spreading fake or conspiracy news in our maps are estimated to be bots or semi-automated accounts.

6. Our maps show that accounts that spread fake news are extremely densely connected.

7. Fake news during the Presidential election did not just adopt conservative or Republican-leaning frames – though it has become more ostensibly Republican since.

8. There are structural changes in the role of Russian-aligned clusters of accounts post-Presidential election.

9. Most of the accounts that linked repeatedly to fake and conspiracy news during the Presidential election are still active.

10. A few dozen accounts controlled by Russia's Internet Research Agency appear in our maps – but hundreds of other accounts were likely more important in spreading fake news.

11. There is evidence of coordinated campaigns to push fake news stories and other types of disinformation.

12. Coordinated campaigns seem to opportunistically amplify content they did not create.

13. One case study suggests that concerted action against noncredible outlets can drastically reduce their audience.

The KF study provides a great deal of insight into the mechanics of Twitter in regard to the spread of mis- or disinformation. In this article, I'd like to offer some limited perspective regarding the specific threats of this type of warfare to supplement the points made in the study. I say "limited" only because influence is far more complex than a short article. Done well, understanding influence is at best a graduate course but, more likely, graduate studies interpreted through a career of implementation.

My definition of an influence campaign such as we have and continue to experience via Russia and other primary threats: Influence done well is a complex and intricate choreography of sustained actions, words and related activities wrapped around a core narrative.

The primary points of the study:

As per the study's first point, this analysis is massive in scope and data driven. One of the most challenging aspects of many of the pieces written regarding social media influence is that while presented by remarkable experts, research must be qualitatively/quantitatively data-driven in order to effectively plan and execute responses. Yes, facts, especially facts, in context matter.

One of the most disturbing findings of the study is that 80 percent of the Twitter accounts disseminating "fake news" are still active. Quantity matters for a variety of reasons. First, reaching as much of an audience possible means a higher probability of triggering the behavior intended. Secondly, and this is a big deal, is that data provides the insights needed to adjust messaging to become more effective. More information (more data) means that the perpetrators can better "tune" the message and learn more about their audience's psychological vulnerabilities. As a frame of reference, this is why the massive amounts of data in the Cambridge Analytica/ Russian fiasco matter.

Data referenced in the third point reveals that the sites hosting/disseminating the most malign messaging still exist. The important point here is that if we were to use the data to implement a proactive and defensive effort, the data points us toward the most dangerous offending sites/ actors. In military terms, knowing where your adversary is and what they're doing provides targeting information. This information is of no value if no significant response is implemented. This, far and above all other points, is most tragic. The U.S., and largely our allies, have no significant strategy and execution to make use of this targeting insight.

Point No. 5 is a critical vulnerability and regards the automation of malign accounts. This is the equivalency of your adversary being massively armed while your forces are not only few in numbers but lightly armed. AI and other automation that amplify adversarial efforts simply means that unless we employ automation that mitigates adversarial automation, our forces will be overwhelmed and rendered ineffective. If we have targeting information regarding automation supported sites, then currently available technology is an effective tool to level the playing field. Current social media platforms primarily focus on identifying individual "bad actors" but largely ignore the originating sites responsible for content and automation. This is often referred to in print as *"whack-a-mole."*

Point No. 6 highlights the ultra-dense centrality of specific sites. "Centrality" in social media terms simply means that of all the malign actors witting or otherwise, are connected to a select few sites responsible for providing the content and connectivity to witting and vulnerable users. Once again, the sites identified through centrality analysis provide targeting information when we decide to mitigate this type of influence. Yes, for those asking about the "800-pound gorilla in the room," Russian efforts are central to these types of sites. For critical reference, I highly recommend following Hamilton 68, a German Marshall Fund Alliance for Securing Democracy project that identifies Russian activity on Twitter in near real-time. Of note, this site also connects Russian Twitter activity to the most prominent websites and URLs responsible for disseminating malign influence on social media. When viewing the Hamilton 68 site, you will no doubt recognize many of the most active URLs/domains since they are prominent U.S. media sites.

The following two points are not only related but are indicative of the "learning" by Russian influencers regarding the potential to effectively influence their targets. While during the 2016 Presidential election a great deal of their effort focused on divisive issues between ideological sides in U.S. politics, post-Presidential election they have evolved toward a more "right-leaning" posture. This evolution demonstrates that they have determined, through analysis, that there is more bang-for-the-buck in these audiences. As with the evolution of U.S. targeting, Russia has learned through success in the U.S. (and, by extension, with UK audiences) that social media/digital influence is worth the investment. Russian activities are now a predominant influence effort in every global arena of value to the Kremlin. To make matters worse, our other primary threats such as Iran, China, North Korea and violent extremist organizations have also absorbed the lessons learned by Russia in the U.S. Presidential election.

Points 10-12 represent one of the most troubling aspects of this study. While Russian accounts are relatively limited, they perform in "lockstep" with hundreds of other, often domestic, accounts. There are countless complicated reasons for this, but the most acute aspect is that Russian accounts provide content to linked accounts. Analysts in Russia also provide analysis to content and responses to content so that they can evolve a message to become more effective at accomplishing their objectives.

This brief analysis merely offers some personal/professional insight into the "so-what" of this study. I'd also like to offer a few thoughts regarding "why" social media is so powerful when applied by influence professionals.

Why is fake news on Twitter and other social media so powerful and what can we do to mitigate its power?

Here's the crux of the matter: social media is the vehicle that transmits influential content. This begs the question: What makes the content so influential?

The answer to this question is complicated – in fact, too much so for a short article like this – but I'll try to pose the answer as succinctly as possible. Humans are tribal by nature. It's simply a matter of who we are. Tribes were formed in order to provide security, sustenance and community. Over a couple hundred thousand years we've evolved, but our DNA still prompts us to reflexively act to sustain our own "tribe." One of the most effective "triggers" to prompt these responses is to threaten or imply a threat to "our tribe." Dividing audiences as a precursor to triggering the threat, implied or otherwise, is a tried-and-true tactic of influencers. Hence, the divisive content favored by Russian "bad actors." The so-called triggers are encoded in our tribal narratives, which is why a full understanding of narrative principles matters to analysis.

To apply narrative principles, analyzing mountains of data that illuminate the narrative identity of their audience is essential. In our current environment, access to these mountains of data is largely provided by hundreds of millions of users so habitually involved in using social media. As noted earlier, Cambridge Analytica, Russia and other adversaries use this data to their advantage and our disadvantage. Simply put, unlocking the specific narrative identity of an audience is the key to being able to predictably trigger "tribally encoded" responses. Advertisers use much the same techniques to get us to buy their products. Yes, we are being manipulated subconsciously every time we log on to a device.

At Narrative Strategies we believe that what Russia and our other adversaries are involved in, to our disadvantage is narrative warfare, not information warfare. The truth is, we are not engaged in a war over information but a war over the meaning of information. Narrative is about meaning, not about truth. As in the KF study, you can see that most tweets are tied in some form to some underlying narrative. Social media and other digital content are the vehicles for delivering content that, based on narrative principles, is designed to predictably trigger responses by users.

So… what does this mean to national security professionals and our citizenry?

Defending the homeland in modern times by default means that we must compete in the cognitive realm. Our conflicts these days are far more about influence than traditional warfare. This means that we need a full spectrum working knowledge of how influence works. Even more important is that we need an information strategy that implements the knowledge of influence. For more on this point, please see this white paper on Homeland Security Today.

As with the final point in the KF executive summary, the situation is not hopeless. There are many actions available to the U.S. government that would and could go a long way toward mitigating Russian and other adversarial influence. The real question is will we employ available knowledge and technology to our defense. Across the spectrum of the U.S. government there are many entities capable of executing pieces of such a strategy. Currently, no entity exists that could effectively lead or conduct such a strategy.

The bottom line is that there is no single tactic or effort that will effectively mitigate this threat. We in the homeland security community must immediately and effectively work together. We are literally within days of our midterm election and we're as prepared as the defenders of the Alamo against overwhelming odds. Courage and tenacity are great but no substitute for being well-armed in the face of a numerically superior and well-armed adversary.

I will also note that outside homeland security and other national security professional communities, every single citizen has the responsibility to be as well-informed as they are activist. Media/digital literacy is a critical component of mitigating outside malign influence. Arming citizens with knowledge is the influence equivalent of a well-armed and trained "national guard." Honest, well-informed citizens are exponentially more capable of not being triggered by the "us vs. them" divisive narratives disseminated by our current threats such as Russia.

Finally, I wish to again thank the Knight Foundation and their colleagues for this extraordinary work. I encourage every single person in the national security arena, cyber, IC, influence or otherwise to read and re-read this study. Strategy is inextricably linked to knowledge. The KF has provided the knowledge. Now, it's up to the U.S. government and our citizenry to apply it.

3

The Government's Failure to Protect the Election

Hold on to your seat. If you are not aware of and familiar with the workings of the national security community, especially DoD, the concepts in this chapter may come as a shock.

First and foremost, it has been decades since the US engaged in what most would consider a conventional war. Nearly all conflicts in modern times are contests with influence being the primary weapon set. Despite the acknowledgement of this aspect of modern conflict by nearly all respected experts, the US national security infrastructure still trains, builds and innovates for conventional war, and with few exceptions, one being, the Special Operations community.

While it is true that a "big stick" military is to some extent deterrence, that alone has not translated to lasting success for the US on most modern battlefields. Deterrence is but one aspect of a wide spectrum of requirements for sustainable, productive influence. Influence is both offensive and defensive. Effective influence is wielding both as required simultaneously. In the ensuing decades, post-Cold War, the US national security community has depended almost exclusively on big budget defense infrastructure as deterrence, a big checkbook and forgotten how to do anything else. The loss of know-how, willingness and a defense structure that could effectively wield influence became the giant hole in our defense that Russia drove through to disrupt our 2016 Presidential elections. Now, China, Iran and many other disrupters and adversaries assault us with weapons of influence around the clock and all year long, while we stand nearly naked and unarmed.

This chapter, written in the Spring of the year 2020, is the *Hail Mary Pass* to call last minute attention to our vulnerability and rally modern "Minutemen" to the parapets. Though this chapter could easily be a book by itself, it's the shortest version I could manage to tell the story of what it means to be unarmed on today's battlefield.

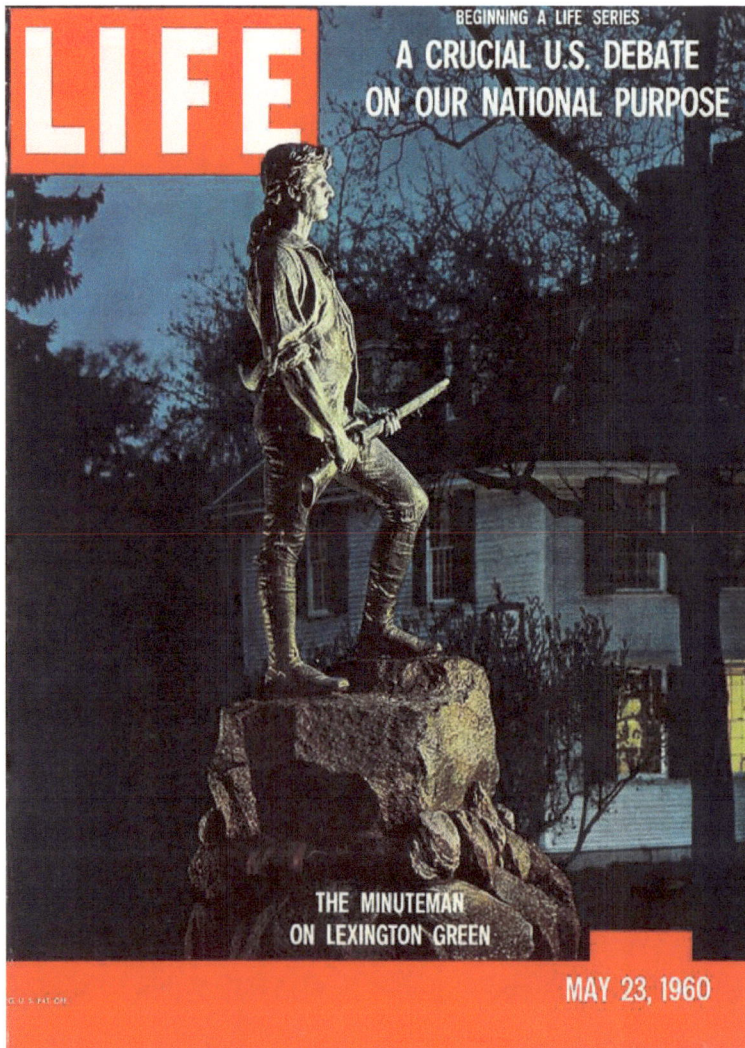

Life Magazine Cover May 23. 1960

Ethical Influence the broken-down, rusting vehicle of American power.

Homeland Security Today Magazine

Published April 2020

Abstract

The US, militarily, is the most powerful nation to ever exist and yet, the single most potent tool in our national security arsenal, lies discarded, broken down and rusting into oblivion. The one thing we did better than anyone else for the past 100 years was to inspire and influence the world based on "who we were". Democratic values vs. fascism was the inspiration for our combined allied victory over Nazi Germany and the AXIS. Freedom based capitalism was the driving factor that welcomed so many allies and partners against communism during the Cold War. Defense of and expansion of human rights has literally been our calling card for decades.

Our success has always been a potent combination of hard and soft power or overall, simply influence. We built capable national security structures and apparatuses to wield influence effectively and ethically. Even as late as the crumbling of the Berlin Wall, the US, in a leadership role was demonstrably effective at ethical influence. Less than a decade later, we had divested ourselves of the knowledge, tools and national security architecture that had paid such handsome rewards during the previous century. In today's world, influence almost exclusively is the battlefield, not terrain and we are unarmed.

Throughout the decades-long ideological struggle with the Soviet Union, we played a leadership role alongside allies and partners opposing Communism. Our success was achieved through a combination of hard and soft power, with the emphasis on the soft. We not only established partnerships and alliances but did the hard work to improve, sustain and grow relationships in order to acquire more influence. With those same partners we robustly executed campaigns to influence at risk nations towards democracy and away from communism. We built resilience at home to prevent the seeds of communism from growing while simultaneously degrading the communist ideology of our adversaries. All of these things and many more are regarded as influence. We not only knew what to do but we energetically campaigned to achieve our objectives. It seems that we've either just plain forgotten how, lack the will or most likely, both.

Every single adversary or competitor from China, Iran and Russia to a variety of extremists are literally dominating the US and our allies/ partners at the moment in the realm of influence. If influence, not terrain is now the primary battlefield, our inaction to compete on the battlefield of influence is literally translated into "executing a full retreat". If we don't compete, we cannot win. If we don't win, we have failed at national security. The gap in our national security arsenal is wide open and ripe for the taking. The purchase of any amount of new ships, tanks and planes cannot fill this massive gap in our national security structure.

A quick scan of the objectives and intentions from the NSS, National Security Strategy, NIS, National Intelligence Strategy and National Defense Strategy do not require a great deal of imagination to see that they are about influence in some form or another. Some of the points even say overtly, "to influence" or "promote" while others hint at such or imply a task that supports influence. You will also note that there are no direct references to "going to war", continuing war in a combat zone etc. Yet... though some points indicate "building or strengthening the force" or "bolstering innovation", there is nothing to suggest that we will build and innovate for being successful at influence. In fact, the current and 2021 budget assessment is replete with misaligned priorities to our current threats.

"At a macro level, the FY 2020 FYDP appears to be inconsistent with the NDS in several respects. Despite the NDS calling for a rebalancing of capabilities to focus more on great power competition and the threats posed by Russia and China, the acquisition budget does not reflect such a shift."

- Analysis of the FY 2020 Defense Budget and Its Implications for FY 2021 and Beyond, CSIS 2/20

A brief survey of our current, prioritized threats such as China, Russia, Iran, N. Korea, and extremism shows that we are not actually at war with any of them other than a CT effort against Islamist extremists in a variety of regions with the outlier being Afghanistan. As of this writing, Afghanistan, by every indication, is winding down in the next few months. Even Afghanistan is no longer a conventional war and as many would argue, me included, it never has been nor should have been.

Influence is literally at the core of every major United States National Security threat. Competition with Russia and China for example is largely via what is termed GPC, great power competition. Simply put, they intend to erode our position of preeminent influence in many regions and nations. The reason that we are leveraging economic sanctions against Iran is influence and also, the on again off again issues with North Korea are a test of wills and leverage, again influence. Of course, building more ships, planes and tanks is deterrence which is its own form of influence but that is not enough as evidenced by Russia's continuing assault on the US through malign influence that is most often associated with our elections. China leverages their economy and partnerships via their Belt and Road Initiative, (BRI) supported by an aggressive military build-up, yes, you guessed it, more influence.

The US National Security Community, especially the Department of Defense seems to believe that simply being the most powerful military in the world is enough influence via deterrence. If this were true, we would not be impacted by Chinese ascendency which targets regional domination by 2035 and global by 2049. If Russia were deterred, they would halt meddling in our domestic affairs and our elections. Iran would stop supplying Hezbollah and supporting Assad in Syria. Extremists would stop executing terrorist attacks and using propaganda to recruit. None of these things are occurring so by default, the gap between the natsec communities' stated positions is demonstrably inconsistent with their actions. It also clearly demonstrates that using only one form of influence, deterrence, is inadequate.

So, when considering the above thoughts, why is there an apparent and dangerous disconnect between our intended NSS and the National Security community's ability to effectively act? The answer is that we long ago lost our former prowess for being able to ethically influence in support of our objectives. We built and expensively sustain a defense architecture geared towards big ticket items and do not invest in the tools, resources, knowledge and infrastructure to accomplish influence. The paradigm is all wrong and everyone with even a modicum of experience in natsec knows it. The problem is that it's just too hard to change... or so our leadership believes.

As we go down the road of attempting to effectively pursue our national security strategy, we're traveling with blinders on and married to risk averse and antiquated thinking. I personally believe that this is because it's just too hard to acknowledge the truth of the changes demanded by our threats. We can do as we did just prior to WWI or WWII and put our head in the sand and wait to adapt after it's too late or... we can use our knowledge and prepare and execute intelligently. Failing to prepare for the challenge at hand has historically cost us dearly. I personally am not a fan of that option, so at risk of angering many in my profession, this article was dedicated to "speaking truth to power".

Introduction

A quick scan of the bullet points beneath this introduction and copied directly from the NSS, NDS and NIS do not require a great deal of imagination to see that they are about influence in some form or another. Some of the points even say overtly, to influence or promote while others hint at such or imply a task that supports influence. You will also note that there are no direct references to going to war, continuing war in a combat zone etc. Yet... though some points indicate building or strengthening the force or bolstering innovation, there is nothing to suggest that we will build and innovate for being successful at influence. In fact, the current and 2021 budget assessment is <u>replete with misaligned priorities to our current threats</u>.

"At a macro level, the FY 2020 FYDP appears to be inconsistent with the NDS in several respects. Despite the NDS calling for a rebalancing of capabilities to focus more on great power competition and the threats posed by Russia and China, the acquisition budget does not reflect such a shift."

- Analysis of the FY 2020 Defense Budget and Its Implications for FY 2021 and Beyond, <u>CSIS 2/20</u>

A brief survey of our current, prioritized threats such as China, Russia, Iran, N. Korea and extremism shows that we are not actually at war with any of them other than a CT effort against Islamist extremists in a variety of regions with the outlier being Afghanistan. As of this writing, Afghanistan, by every indication, is winding down in the next few months. Even Afghanistan is no longer a conventional war and as many would argue, me included, it never has been nor should have been.

Influence is literally at the core of every major US natsec threat. Competition with Russia and China for example is largely via what is termed GCP, **great power competition.** Simply put, they intend to erode our position of preeminent influence in many regions and nations. The reason that we are leveraging economic sanctions against Iran is influence and also, the on again/ off again issues with N. Korea are a test of wills and leverage, again influence. Of course, building more ships, planes and tanks is deterrence which is its own form of influence but that is not enough as evidenced by Russia's continuing assault on the US through malign influence that is most often associated with our elections. China leverages their economy and partnerships via their **Belt and Road Initiative, (BRI)** supported by an aggressive military build-up, yes, you guessed it, more influence.

It would seem that the US natsec community, especially DOD seems to believe that simply being the most powerful military in the world is enough influence via deterrence. If this were true, we would not be impacted by Chinese ascendency which targets regional domination by 2035 and global by 2049. If Russia were deterred, they would halt meddling in our domestic affairs and our elections. Iran would stop supplying Hezbollah and supporting Assad in Syria. Extremists would stop executing terrorist attacks and using propaganda to recruit. None of these things are occurring so by default, the gap between the natsec communities' stated positions is demonstrably inconsistent with their actions. It also clearly **demonstrates that using only one form of influence, deterrence, is inadequate.**

So, when considering the above thoughts, why is there an apparent and dangerous disconnect between our intended NSS and the natsec community's ability to effectively act? The answer is that we long ago lost our former prowess for being able to ethically influence in support of our objectives. We built and expensively sustain a defense architecture geared towards big ticket items and do not invest in the tools, resources, knowledge and infrastructure to accomplish influence. The paradigm is all wrong and everyone with even a modicum of experience in natsec knows it. The problem is that it's just too hard to change… or so our leadership believes.

What follows is a discussion of our most significant deficiencies, some recommendations, and a call to action for those entrusted with the sacred duty to protect our nation. Again, this is constructive criticism intended to chart a course that is effective, responsive and sustainable in modern warfare that is best characterized as a competition of wills rather than big ticket military hardware.

Before we proceed, please take a look at the objectives of the 3 named national security documents below: 1. <u>NSS, National Security Strategy</u>, 2. <u>NIS, National Intelligence Strategy</u> and our 3. <u>National Defense Strategy</u>

<u>**NSS** objectives:</u>

1. First, our fundamental responsibility is to protect the American people, the homeland, and the American way of life. We will strengthen control of our borders and reform our immigration system. We will protect our critical infrastructure and go after malicious cyber actors.

2. Second, we will promote American prosperity. We will rejuvenate the American economy for the benefit of American workers and companies. We will insist upon fair and reciprocal economic relationships to address trade imbalances.

3. Third, we will preserve peace through strength by rebuilding our military so that it remains preeminent, deters our adversaries, and if necessary, is able to fight and win. We will compete with all tools of national power to ensure that regions of the world are not dominated by one power

4. Fourth, we will advance American influence because a world that supports American interests and reflects our values makes America more secure and prosperous. We will compete and lead in multilateral organizations so that American interests and principles are protected.

NDS Objectives:

1. Defending the homeland from attack.

2. Sustaining Joint Force military advantages, both globally and in key regions;

3. Deterring adversaries from aggression against our vital interests;

4. Enabling U.S. interagency counterparts to advance U.S. influence and interests;

5. Maintaining favorable regional balances of power in the Indo-Pacific, Europe, the Middle East, and the Western Hemisphere.

6. Defending allies from military aggression and bolstering partners against coercion, and fairly sharing responsibilities for common defense;

7. Dissuading, preventing, or deterring state adversaries and non-state actors from   acquiring, proliferating, or using weapons of mass destruction;

8. Preventing terrorists from directing or supporting external operations against the United States homeland and our citizens, allies, and partners overseas.

9. Ensuring common domains remain open and free.

10. Continuously delivering performance with affordability and speed as we change

11. Departmental mindset, culture, and management systems; and

12. Establishing an unmatched twenty-first century National Security Innovation Base that effectively supports Department operations and sustains security and solvency.

<u>**NIS**</u> objectives or "must dos":

1. Increase integration and coordination of our intelligence activities to achieve best effect and value in executing our mission,

2. Bolster innovation to constantly improve our work,

3. Better leverage strong, unique, and valuable partnerships to support and enable national security outcomes, and

4. Increase transparency while protecting national security information to enhance accountability and public trust.

The Role of Influence in National Security Strategy

The premise of this paper is that we, the US, along with allies and partners, have insufficient natsec architecture, will and available knowledge to influence in support of our natsec objectives ethically and effectively. So, what is this mysterious thing called "influence"?

The Merriam-Webster Dictionary's #1 definition

Definition of *influence*

1: "the power or capacity of causing an effect in indirect or intangible ways "

My version of a definition for influence relative to this paper:

"Influence, done well is achieved by a complex and intricate choreography of sustained actions, words and related activities wrapped around a core narrative that continually modifies behavior in a manner supportive of natsec objectives."

The NWC, National War College/ NDU, National Defense University primer states in the overview in chapter 1 that;

"Fundamentally, national security strategy entails the design and application of ideas for employment of means as well as the orchestration of institutions and instruments of national power (diplomatic, informational, military, and economic) to achieve viable ends that protect or advance national interests. National security strategy bridges the gap from a less-desirable current state of affairs or condition to a more desirable future state of affairs or condition. National security strategy can apply broadly, organizing or guiding nearly all aspects of a state's policy, or more narrowly regarding a specific situation. Conceptually, national security generally entails the competitive search for advantage over a foreign nation, group of nations, or non-state actor; a favorable foreign relations position; and/or a defense posture capable of successfully deterring hostile action."

Though less succinct than the dictionary definition, the **NWC primer speaks directly to influence as the primary tool of US national security strategy.** Notable also is that it says directly that such influence is the "orchestration of institutions and instruments of national power (diplomatic, informational, military, and economic)". The key word in this key phrase is "orchestration" and still, nearly 4 decades after the fall of the Soviet Union and when the US and our allies/ partners effectively participated in such orchestration, the US no longer has a natsec architecture capable of achieving effective influence. Simply put, the tools of "orchestration" either no longer exist or have been replaced by a plethora of meetings, working groups and ad hoc boards that lack the ability to actually do anything other than talk about the problems.

Did we assume that influence would become akin to bows and arrows, muskets etc.? Did we believe that leading a unipolar world would only require demonstrable military power and the world's largest economy? These and a host of other pertinent questions are at the heart of our problem. The common expression that many would recognize in their daily lives is that we became **not only complacent but inattentive**.

US Influence Actors

This topic is a complicated one and for a variety of reasons. The short answer is~everyone, every agency or entity does this, but in theory only. The reason that this is "theory only is that orchestration is effectively non-existent. The long answer is much more difficult and takes some explaining.

First and foremost, we must know what we are influencing in support of. The NSS articulates this but in actuality, it is currently up to disparate elements of the USG to decide on their own how or if they can or will support it.

Inside the Beltway, DOS, Department of State and within the leadership of their regional bureaus, public policy agendas are discussed for implementation. DOD does much the same via the Pentagon and GCCs, Global Combatant Commands such as CENTCOM or AFRICOM, etc. Both DOS and DOD along with other USG entities attend an endless array of meetings to discuss influence strategy and execution. **The hard truth though is that despite all these coordinating entities and meetings, the amount of actual campaigning that is derived from these meetings is negligible at best, ineffective at worst. This isn't because there is an absence of talent and intelligence but largely due to the oppressive weight of bureaucracy, risk averse leadership and an absence of an effective coordinating mechanism that can act on those decisions and has what is called 'tasking authority".** Tasking authority simply means that someone is in charge that has the authority to tell others what to do.

Although DOS and DOD are the first to come to mind when discussing influence strategy, they are hardly the only two worth discussing. Nearly every single US agency in some way or other also has connectivity with those outside US borders. As I often explained to commanders when deployed and executing influence campaigns, "anyone or anything that engages with my target audience is capable of influencing them".

The Department of Agriculture for example has the FAS, Foreign Agricultural Service whose primary task is to engage foreign nations regarding markets and food security. This agency by default has excellent influence with foreign nations due to what is stated in their mission statement.

The Department of Education has the Bureau of Educational and Cultural Affairs which *"provides an avenue for students to foster long-lasting ties with people around the globe, promote mutual understanding, develop leadership skills, and enhance educational achievements."* It would be difficult to interpret this intent as anything but influence.

The Departments of Agriculture and Education examples are but two of countless USG engagements with the outside world and every single one is an opportunity to support our NSS objectives but… they are very rarely if ever incorporated into National Security planning and execution. The operative question here is why? We will get around to answering this question a bit later in this paper.

During the Cold War, the US had the USIA, US Information Agency which largely was responsible for coordinating USG efforts to combat the influence of the USSR and promote US democratic values. Many of the other agencies of the US government played a role in our wide-spectrum anti-communism campaigning, verbally and by actions. While not perfect it did provide a mechanism for coordinating US influence. With its demise in the late 1990s, we no longer have any such mechanism.

There are now plenty of ad hoc efforts or even officially designated entities but not one single one has either the political capital or funding to achieve comprehensive effects.

DOS, Department of State

The lead for US foreign policy obviously is DOS. There are multiple entities within DOS that coordinate, analyze, and make recommendations for the implementation of US foreign policy. Each and every one has missions that somehow speak to influence in support of US objectives, including the NSS. In theory, with so many bright professionals focused on successful implementation of US policy one would think that we would make more progress than the negligible amount we currently see. Like DoD and other agencies, the lack of progress is not for lack of talent, but something that you will read often in this paper, **a lack of an effective mechanism across the spectrum of the USG for orchestrating policy.**

DOS does though do the best they can to at least synchronize within themselves, despite limited resources. For example; "the Under Secretary for Public Diplomacy and Public Affairs serves as the lead policy maker for the Department's overall public outreach and press strategies, whether conducted virtually or in-person." This is the team that keeps US foreign policy messaging and support synchronized at least within DOS and with the intention of wider synchronization.. The public affairs efforts here are key to ensuring that the decisions made by Ambassadors and other affiliated senior leaders are presented in a manner that supports the overarching US NSS and its regional and country specific outreach. **Of course, this would be more effective with an overarching narrative strategy, not just at State**

73

but at even higher levels, which it doesn't. Still, this office does the hard work of attempting to synchronize engagement with the outside world so that everyone both understands our intent and isn't confused by it. The <u>Bureau of Global Public Affairs</u>, are the actual voices of that effort.

DOS, arguably a critical factor in the US's ability to ethically influence, currently has <u>problems just managing day to day business due to funding reductions, staffing issues and morale.</u> The GEC, Global Engagement Center is charged with leading US strategic influence efforts both offensive and defensive but other than close relationships with other partners such as DOD, has few resources available. To be fair, the GEC's primary function is to coordinate and synchronize but still, without a mechanism for effective operational control even their leadership is insufficient to address their mission. A key phrase in the vision portion of their mission statement is **"proactively address"** but again, if those sitting together with the GEC do not take a proactive approach, all the synchronizing, analysis and recommendations come to naught.

CD/ Critical deficiencies at DOS

DOS, specifically the Ambassador who is the president's personal representative in a nation is literally the face of America in foreign countries. Nothing can occur via US agencies or companies without the Ambassador's approval. The short version of why this is important is that relative to US strategic objectives, there must be focused coordination to ensure that any US entity working in a nation is working towards our strategic objectives which include those articulated in our NSS. The Amb. is literally the arbiter of US interests. In theory, this means that NSS is part of their portfolio. The Amb. and embassy staff must be well aware of and pursue through the Amb's vision the tenets of our strategy. This is rarely an issue with career FSO's (foreign service officers) but as with all administrations, **political appointees often fail to see the whole picture.**

In regards to direct influence, the <u>GEC, Global Engagement Center</u> at DOS is charged:

"To direct, lead, synchronize, integrate, and coordinate efforts of the Federal Government to recognize, understand, expose, and counter foreign state and non-state propaganda and disinformation efforts aimed at undermining or influencing the policies, security, or stability of the United States, its allies, and partner nations."

The GEC, as can be seen by their mission statement is at the heart of the fight regarding foreign influence targeting the US and partners. Like DoD and other US entities, the GEC is staffed by talented, forward thinkers. They interact with all of the primary participants in their mission efforts. They host excellent analysis and in fact share effectively with their partners. As for "leading", **they are hobbled, like everyone else by the weight of bureaucracy and lack of tasking authorities.**

The primary problem when it comes to fighting foreign malign influence, is that one of the most effective approaches is <u>resiliency</u>. For an entity "leading" our efforts, they have little to no role at all in hardening targets within the US. Just sharing with our allies and partners isn't enough. As demonstrated by our 2016 Presidential elections and continued foreign efforts, our population is the target most in need of "hardening".

The other primary issue hobbling the GEC being effective is that those they partner with, and in particular DoD are risk averse, resource starved and fail to actually campaign with the knowledge shared at the GEC table.

Finally, considering the fine work done by analysts at the GEC and their partners, their public website is barren with information regarding that analysis. **They, as the lead agency for protecting the US from malign foreign influence must make an unclassified version of analysis available to the public so that anyone searching their page could access that analysis.** This would be especially helpful to organizations and local governments who cannot participate in briefings, VTCs or events. Again, **knowledge is useless unless in the hands of those who need it and will actually put that knowledge to work**. Foreign influence is a battlefield and must be treated as such. Just imagine what would happen if every military member in a combat zone didn't have access to their weapons.

The bullets, quotes and linked reports below articulate better than I ever could some of the biggest challenges for success in the DOS mission:

- First and foremost, under the current administration, DOS has seen a 30% reduction in staff which hampers its potential to do anything more than merely keep up with its day to day tasks.

- Along with staff reductions have come significant funding decreases. USAID which is one of our long used and most effective tools for partnership and influence in partner nations has seen some of the most draconic cuts.

"On March 11, 2019, the Trump Administration proposed its FY2020 budget for the Department of State, Foreign Operations, and Related Programs (SFOPS) accounts, which fund U.S. diplomatic activities, cultural exchanges, development and

security assistance, and U.S. participation in multilateral organizations, among other international activities."

- CRS report: Department of State, Foreign Operations, and Related Programs: FY2020 Budget and Appropriations Updated March 12, 2020

"State, Foreign Operations, and Related Programs (SFOPS) accounts, which fund U.S. diplomatic activities, cultural exchanges, development and security assistance, and U.S. participation in multilateral organizations, among other international activities was lower than any SFOPS funding level in the last decade"

-CRS report: Department of State, Foreign Operations, and Related Programs: FY2020 Budget and Appropriations Updated March 12, 2020

The State Department's mission is compromised by "staff shortages, frequent turnover, poor leadership, and inexperienced and under trained staff," the department's inspector general warned in a new report.

"Workforce management issues are pervasive, affecting programs and operations domestically and overseas and across functional areas and geographic regions," the watchdog reported Wednesday.

- Inspector General Statement on the Department of State's Major Management and Performance Challenges FISCAL YEAR 2019

Department of Defense

As always, let's start with where we are now. First and foremost, DoD has long been uncomfortable with the word influence, preferring other doctrinal terms like IO, Information Operations or IW, Information Warfare. Regardless of what DoD calls their efforts, they are currently and have been for decades, best described as and the reason for the title to this paper; "**Operationally Ineffective**". The Pentagon's efforts at influence could easily be portrayed as a <u>Rube Goldberg machine</u>, something relatively famous in my youth. **A Rube Goldberg machine is an intricate, overly complicated contraption capable of only carrying out a simple task.**

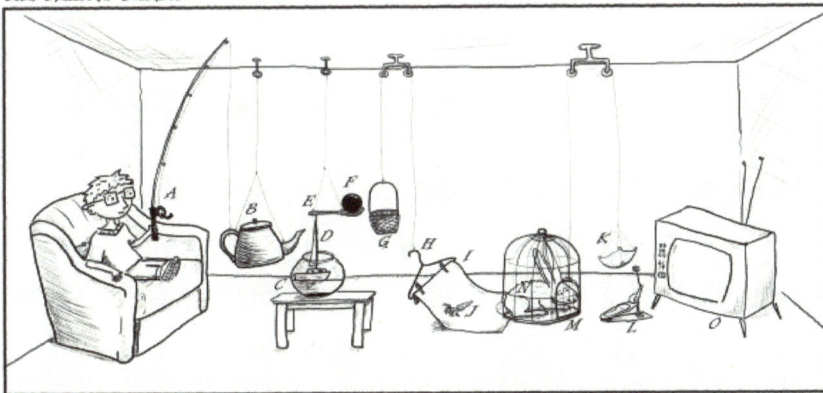

Invention of the week - no. 55
The Remote Control

Boy sitting on couch reels in fishing rod (A) causing kettle (B) to tilt and pour water into fish bowl (C). As water level rises, toy yacht (D) floats higher and tilts spoon (E) causing ball (F) to roll into basket (G). As basket drops to floor, coat hanger (H) rises making towel (I) stretch tight and baby carrot (J) is launched through the air. As carrot lands in napkin (K), it falls gently onto bass drum pedal (L) and causes door of rabbit cage (M) to open. Rabbit (N) comes out of cage to eat carrot and steps on bass drum pedal causing pedal to strike the power button on television (O) allowing boy to enjoy the show.

PHOTOSHOPTALENT.COM

IO doctrinal changes and considerations over the past decade or so have been overwhelmingly focused on tinkering with the machinery of their *IO Rube Goldberg* machine rather than finding a way to actually make it more effective and do more than a simple task.

As the only entity within the USG with an allegedly organized system capable of influence across the spectrum of activities required in my definition above, is DOD. As this is my personal area of expertise, I will offer more insight here.

The format for what follows regarding DoD will be, first to understand what IO looks like and then to take a look at critical deficiencies, **which will be in bold and underlined.**

What is IO?

IO, the acronym for Information Operations, which is somewhat evolving into IW, Information Warfare doctrinally is primarily where influence is nested at DoD. It is part of operations and its mission, architecture etc. is laid out in JOINT PUB, 3-13. Although this publication is being re-written, here's the DoD definition of record; "*the integrated employment, during military operations, of information-related capabilities in concert with other lines of operation to influence, disrupt, corrupt, or usurp the decision making of adversaries and potential adversaries while protecting our own*".

From a lay perspective most are wondering just what in the hell does this mean? As a longtime member of this community, I have often wondered the same. Scrolling through the 80 + pages of J 3-13, I doubt that any reader not well-versed in military doctrine will understand the relationship of the doctrine to influencing in support of natsec objectives. In an era where DoD supports natsec in operations far from kinetic battlefields and in conjunction with partner forces, civilian agencies and more, **simple, clearly articulated concepts are more important than doctrine written by and for those who do so.** To be fair, most who write IO doctrines are some of the best and brightest but are also victims of a system that speaks more to itself than to users.

This is a good time in this paper to advance what many consider a radical concept; "Influence is not part of operations, it is operations." Even in the heat of a pitched battle between adversaries, the intent is to influence the other side to give up, alter their strategy in a manner beneficial to your side or a variety of other effects. Overwhelming force is convincing but so is deception, undermining the morale of the opponent, confusing opposing commanders to your strength and position etc. No matter what the military does, there is at least one intended effect that can be best accomplished by doing multiple things or not, simultaneously. To do this well, doctrine must be much more focused, streamlined, integrated and easily explained. The current hieroglyphics of IO doctrine is not capable of this.

In my days as an IO practitioner in uniform, I never used IO doctrinal language to brief a commander that I was seeking approval from to execute influence. I had learned early on that **busy commanders whether in tactical, operational or strategic roles didn't have time to decipher what IO doctrinal language means**. They simply wanted to know in basic terms if it could be done, was it legal and could I demonstrate that it worked? The IO community, mistakenly assumed to be versed in influence, had failed the first rule, "they failed to understand their audience" when staffing.

For any organization to be able to influence, it must be as practiced, trained and agile as our finest special operations forces. It must be able to adapt in real-time as well as it does long range planning and execution. It must interact with partners responsively. Simply put, it must be as influential as it is lethal.

The next portion of this paper will be to address what I consider to be the **five most critical deficiencies** within DoD regarding being effective in influence. Were there time, there could be at least 50 but for the purpose of making the salient points as succinctly as possible, we'll stick with 5.

CD/ Critical Deficiencies at DoD

1st CD: coordination, staffing and tasking authority

In the past three decades, the US has relied far too heavily on the US military to do its bidding in engagement outside our borders regarding influence. Someone in uniform has all too often been the only or most prominent face of America during times when our influence has been most needed. This is not to say that other agencies/ entities have not participated, because they most certainly have. The problem though in places like the Middle East, all parts of Asia, Africa, South America, Europe etc. is that there has been no effective method for synchronizing the efforts of our <u>instruments of national power</u> when they were participating. To this point, <u>JDN (JOINT Doctrine Note) 1-18 on page II 8,</u> describes the importance of and the requirement for the means but does not identify such. **The lack of ability to identify the means for orchestration is a gap that is cavernous and the first aspect of the DoD portion of this paper that we will take a look at.**

Per the earlier definition that I use for influence, DoD is the only USG entity that can control multiple elements capable of exerting it at one time… or can they? For this reason, outside US borders DoD is often seen as the lead department. In combat zones and/ or failed states, this is often a responsible and pragmatic answer. The problem is, in current form, it is not capable.

*"Influence, done well is achieved by a complex and intricate choreography of sustained actions, words and related activities wrapped around a **core narrative** that continually modifies behavior in a manner supportive of natsec objectives."*

-Paul Cobaugh , 2016

Before proceeding, it is important for non-military readers to understand that like many nations, the US military operates on three different levels; strategic, operational and tactical. There are multiple layers of staffing at each level.

DoD is organized in a byzantine manner that creates "fiefdoms" called GCCs, Global Combatant Commands. Each commander, much like a feudal lord has enormous power on their own turf. One of the problems though is that most of our prominent threats span multiple or all GCCs such as dealing with China and her global ascendency. If we are to effectively coordinate influence activities as part of a NSS-centric strategy, such coordination becomes overly difficult. Commanders in a sense "own" the resources and assets assigned to them. Often, there is not enough to go around and each CDR has to be willing and able to relinquish resources. This is not always practical or doable. The Pentagon in the past handful of years has tinkered with new concepts to improve on this but to date, nothing of value has come from any such effort.

To make matters worse, each command and supporting command has their own layers of staff and resources assigned. Coordination between the top, down to individual commands is best portrayed as the childhood game of playing "telephone". By the time plans, products and ideas go up and down the different levels of staffing, they often are dramatically different than the original. As an example, let's say that a local commander in Somalia has a PSYOP team with a great idea; that idea filters up through every layer of staffing locally and then back to the US where it also goes through multiple layers of staffing. By the time a response comes back down to the original team, it has been edited, hacked at, chopped on watered down to be almost ineffective or obsolete due to the time it took to staff.

Anecdotally, as an IO practitioner in Afghanistan working for a Special Operations TF (task force), if I used US influence tools, which are called 'capabilities", there were very few times that I received timely and locally relevant support. If I walked across the road and used local NATO support, I had exactly what I wanted and nearly always within a day. It wasn't that my US providers weren't good at their job but due to staffing requirements and too many "edits"/ suggestions, products became watered down and were absent the local insights required to be effective. Often, the length of time it took to even receive these made those products irrelevant because of the long development/ staffing time.

At the strategic level, coordination between the Pentagon and the GCCs is even worse and rarely produces anything of value to either. The Pentagon who is primarily responsible for strategic influence, is also the home to our **next critical deficiency; STRATCOMS**.

Finally, under this topic the most serious coordination issue is that IO/ IW doesn't own any resources or assets. It is literally a "mother, may I?" situation where commanders cannot control/ task what needs to be done to support their mission. It's up to the IO planners to get everyone together, create a plan and then hope that all of the required tools (IRCs) will commit what is required, in the manner requested and at the time needed.

The daunting conclusion to this section is that the architecture of IO is maddeningly over-complicated, confusing, not practiced the same everywhere and in desperate need of a full overhaul.

As a visual example of just how confusing IO doctrine can be are the two graphics below. As a practitioner, they still baffle me.

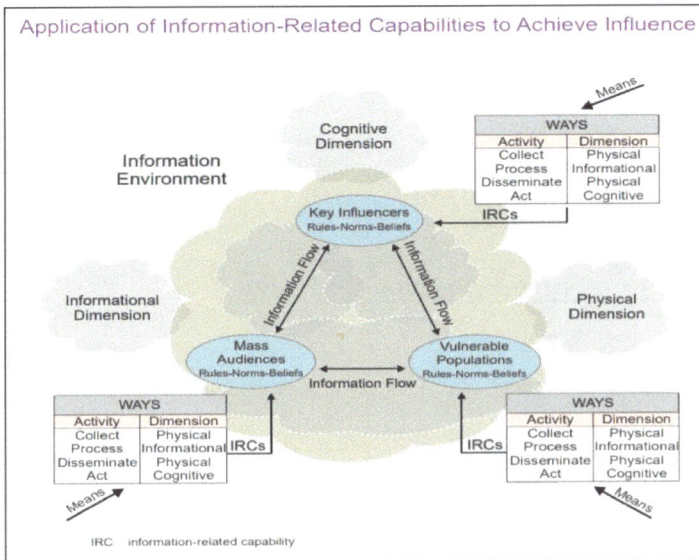

Figure I-4. Application of Information-Related Capabilities to Achieve Influence

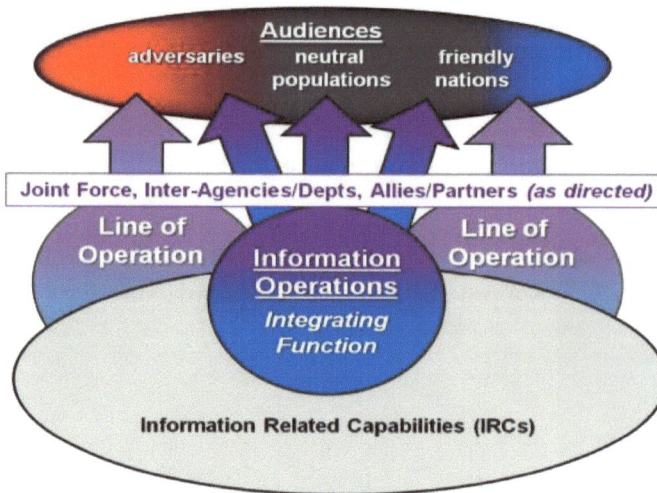

IO Employment of IRCs

2nd CD: Little or no Strategic Communications

First, let's get a couple of definitions in place before we wade into this topic. I want to also note that while this particular discussion is under the DoD heading, much also applies to the rest of the USG as well, particularly at the most senior levels.

What is SC, Strategic Communications? There are several definitions of this term, some succinct and some overly involved. As an example of a sound non-military version, I like Chatham House's version: "*A systematic series of sustained and coherent activities, conducted across strategic, operational and tactical levels, that enables understanding of target audiences and, identifies effective conduits to promote and sustain particular types of behaviour.*" (Please note the similarities here to my articulated definition of influence above)

NATO uses the term "STRATCOM" and it is slightly different but in important ways for military applications. It is defined as: "*There are many definitions that define Strategic Communications. The current NATO approved definition of Strategic Communications says that Strategic Communication is the coordinated and appropriate use of NATO communications activities and capabilities - Public Diplomacy, Public Affairs, Military Public Affairs, Information Operations and Psychological Operations, as appropriate - in support of Alliance policies, operations and activities, and in order to advance NATO's aims."*

<u>DoD: Strategic Communication Joint Integrating Concept</u> *Strategic communication is the alignment of multiple lines of operation (e.g., policy implementation, public affairs, force movement, information operations etc.) that together generate effects to support national objectives. Strategic communication essentially means sharing meaning (i.e., communicating) in support of national objectives (i.e., strategically). This involves listening as much as transmitting and applies not only to information, but also physical communication—action that conveys meaning.*

What is far more important here than arguing the wordsmithing of definitions is the absence of STRACOMS from the USG and especially at DoD. In 2012, DoD abandoned SC and wove their job into Public Affairs and other functions such as IO where none of those functions are accomplishing the SC mission. Truth be told, DoD is best suited in a supporting role for SC but the USG as a whole, other than the GEC and a handful of PAOs and senior leaders is disconnected and lacks both a synchronizing mechanism and a robust effort.

For the sake of simplicity, let's assume SC should be the virtual backbone of the USG's efforts to communicate the meaning of our words and actions around the globe via narrative-centric outreach. Meaning is crucial so that allies, partners and adversaries are not confused about US intentions. The result is chaos, indecision and distrust. No paper that discusses DoD would be

87

complete without a *Sun Tzu quote* and this one applies here; **"there is opportunity in chaos"**. This may be true for those skilled in strategy, well-organized and with sound leadership but this is not the current case within DoD when it comes to SC, IO or anything else, influence related. **The only influence tool with the potential to resolve chaos in influence campaigns is narrative.**

3rd CD: A lack of understanding regarding narrative

The problem within DoD, like most USG public communications groups is that most don't understand what narrative is. This makes it nearly impossible to develop and execute a narrative-centric influence campaign, even if an effective organization existed.

War is a contest for influence. This contest occurs in narrative space that contains terrain and has morphology. Organizations, nonstate actors and states operate throughout the narrative space to influence partners and opponents to accomplish their interests.

-Brian Steed

Narrative strategy is critical as the core of any influence campaign because it confers meaning on what audiences see, hear and experience. **If we don't offer a meaning, our adversaries most certainly will.** Once a narrative is established, it is exceptionally difficult to defeat. The only thing that beats an existing, established narrative is a more compelling, alternative narrative. **Counter-narratives alone do not work** but are valuable in a complete strategy that includes both offensive and defensive narratives.

At the moment, the truth is that we are engaged in narrative warfare with Russia, China, extremists and many more, not Information Warfare.

We are not engaged in an information war;

we are engaged in a war over the meaning of information.

-Dr. Ajit Maan, 2018

Let's start with the basics and build from there; What is narrative?

Narrative is as natural to human beings as breathing. We are meaning-seeking animals and our primary means of meaning-making is narrative. Narrative is the way we create, transmit, and in some cases, negotiate meaning. Without narrative, life would be experienced as an unconnected and overwhelming series of random events. We organize, prioritize, and order our experiences through narratives that we usually inherit. What's more, we understand not only the world around us, but also ourselves, through the narratives we live by; our personal narratives inform our personal identities, our tribal/familial narratives inform our tribal/familial identities, and our national narratives inform our national identity.

-Dr. Ajit Maan 2018

Our Think/ Do Tank, *Narrative Strategies*, uses the following equation when instructing natsec community members about narrative:

The primary construct of narrative: NARRATIVE = Meaning + Identity + Content + Structure ©

Meaning: Narratives do not necessarily tell the truth, they give meaning to a succession of events, facts (real or otherwise). That does not necessarily imply that narratives involve patent dishonesty although they may. It does though mean that when narrative is presented based on the art and science of narrative it does not allow the audience to derive their own meaning. The narrator (s) control this.

Identity: Literally, who someone or some group is. All people and groups, families, tribes, clubs, nations, religious entities etc. have specific identities unique to them. Within a group, not all are precisely the same but have shared "layers" of identity.

Content: The facts, pieces of information (true or not) the story/ narrative is built around. Remember, narrative gives meaning to the information included in the story.

Structure: The way the content is told is the form or structure of the narrative. The most recognized Western structure is the one outlined by Aristotle, that which has a beginning, a middle, and an end. Not all cultures share this structure, particularly outside the Western world.

Every single TA, target audience has its own unique NI, **narrative identity**. Each TA also communicates in their own unique way **structurally**. Whatever the **meaning** intended to be communicated and based on the **content** must take NI and structure into consideration or risk ending up with a confused TA. For experienced open-source analysts, it's far more common than not to see that our allies and partners, as well as our adversaries are more confused than less by US statements and actions. Speeches, PRs, press releases are not enough unless they are built on narrative principles and are used to engage each unique audience actively and persistently. In other words, we must

90

campaign by keeping narrative principles at the core of every effort, without exception.

To build and orchestrate a narrative-centric influence campaign requires forms of INTEL collection and analysis outside of existing disciplines. None of the existing INTEL disciplines collect in the categories noted in the equation; N=M+I+C+S. It is only logical that if you do not learn to collect and analyze the required information, you cannot develop an effective narrative-centric campaign.

Another significant and long-recognized/ unaddressed deficiency is the ability to effectively assess the success of failure of influence campaigns. Again, types of collection represent the primary obstacle. In a country that has *Madison Avenue*, synonymous with modern advertising, it is almost unfathomable that DoD cannot tap into the expertise for assessing the effectiveness of campaigns.

To put things into a summarized perspective from this critical deficiency please think long and hard on the following;

If we accept the premise that influence is; *"is achieved by a complex and intricate choreography of sustained actions, words and related activities wrapped around a core narrative that continually modifies behavior in a manner supportive of natsec objectives"* then by default, explaining the meaning of those words and actions is the critical piece of our strategy. **As noted, if we don't explain our meaning, our adversaries will and if they are first and convincing, it's nearly impossible to alter that narrative.** Furthermore, without transmitting meaning both our adversaries and our allies will be confused to our intent, a fatal flaw.

Narrative, done well and built on solid narrative principles is the only mechanism of influence that transmits meaning simply because that is how humans have always conferred meaning. It's literally in our DNA.

One overarching narrative is not enough. A narrative-centric strategy requires a what we call a **FON, family of narratives** that incorporate the full spectrum of offensive and defensive narratives.

Understanding the principles of narrative and their practical "how to" applications falls into the category of training and tradecraft which will be our next CD, critical deficiency.

4th CD, antiquated and ineffective training and tradecraft

In regard to training and tradecraft, DoD, the only entity with an alleged system for influence is overwhelmingly deficient. In an extensive RAND 2012 study of IO and related activities in Afghanistan, Dr. Arturo Munoz and Erin Dick "concluded that there was a disconnect between the doctrine and practice of information operations (IO) in the field that was counterproductive to effective and efficient operations."

Key Finding from this report:

*While there have been some tactical IO successes in Afghanistan, **little progress has been made in the area of doctrine integration and harmonization** and the establishment of measures of effectiveness in the five years since the previous study period ended (2010).*

This deficiency will have an even greater negative impact as the United States continues to reduce the number of troops in theater and as resources to combat the enemy's propaganda offence remain limited.

In a report released in conjunction with the RAND IO analysis listed above, RAND issued a report on <u>PSYOP effectiveness in Afghanistan</u> that was also far less than favorable. The highlights are as follow:

Key findings:

- *Efforts to win the support of the Afghan population for U.S. and allied military operations have had mixed success.*

- *The most successful initiatives were those involving face-to-face communication.*

- *The most notable shortcoming was the inability to effectively counter Taliban propaganda against U.S. and NATO forces regarding civilian casualties.*

- ***Inadequate coordination, long response times for message approval, and an inability to exploit informal, oral communication were among the most significant problems with these initiatives***.

<u>Graphic from the RAND report:</u>

Assessment of Major Themes in Psychological Operations in Afghanistan

Theme	Assessment
The war on terror justifies U.S. intervention.	Ineffective
Coalition forces bring peace and progress.	Effective (2001–2005); Mixed (2006–2010)
Al-Qai'da and the Taliban are enemies of the Afghan people.	Mixed
Monetary rewards are offered for the capture of al-Qai'da and Taliban leaders.	Ineffective
Monetary rewards are offered for turning in weapons.	Mixed
Support of local Afghans is needed to eliminate improvised explosive devices.	Mixed
U.S. forces have overwhelming technological superiority over the Taliban.	Effective (2001–2005); Mixed (2006–2010)
The Government of the Islamic Republic of Afghanistan and Afghan National Security Forces bring peace and progress.	Mixed
Democracy benefits Afghanistan, and all Afghans need to participate in elections.	Effective (2001–2005); Mixed (2006–2010)

To further the point that connects training to effectiveness, <u>Dr. Montgomery McFate writes</u>;

"Socio-cultural analysis shops, such as the Strategic Studies Detachment of 4th Psychological Operations Group and the Behavioral Influences Analysis Division of the National Air and Space Intelligence Center, are underfunded, marginalized, and dispersed. Because they lack resources, their information base is often out of date."

-Dr. Montgomery McFate

Dr. Thomas Johnson, of Naval Postgraduate School and author of Taliban Narratives is more pointed regarding the failure of the US generally and the IO/ PSYOP community to effectively integrate culture into their campaigns, writing;

IO efforts were examined using the U.S. PSYOP Book from 2009. The analyses concluded with the notion that the U.S. had to basically surrender to Taliban dominance in narratives and associated stories. The U.S. efforts basically refused to accept Afghan cultural reality

-Professor Thomas Johnson

In the voluminous PSYOP handbook an attempt to search it will reveal that the word culture is referenced 31 times and yet, as we have seen in the RAND study and other comments, this is still one of the organization's most significant flaws. For an influence organization that operates outside US borders, this is not only a deficit but a fatal flaw.

I will add that, in my long experience as a practitioner with more than a handful of deployments, Cultural intelligence across the spectrum of DoD and other entities operating in combat zones is generally poor. There are exceptions such as within certain SOF, Special Operations Forces communities but I repeat, these are the exceptions. I spent part of each year for 5 successive years (2009-1013) in Afghanistan as an IO officer. It wasn't until after the first and the only deployment attempting to employ doctrinal approaches, that I found success. Success came in the form of pragmatism and most of all, putting local culture at the core of my efforts. Doctrine and process didn't work then and sadly, still doesn't.

An issue that DoD absolutely must address and goes to the heart of the failure to influence is the concept of the person responsible for making influence happen, the "IO Planner". IO is seen exclusively by DoD as a staff job whose purpose is to bring together doctrinal pieces/ tools called IRCs (information related capabilities) and work towards a plan that synchronizes the tools that the IRCs can bring to bear. These tools are narrowly defined by doctrine and often not "owned" by the local commander. In short, the experts get together and pose suggestions of what their respective IRCs can do and then have to go back and ask if those that own the resources can and will participate in the manner recommended. To say this system is unwieldy and unproductive would be far too kind.

Whether it's the Army's IO "schoolhouse" or the JOINT Staff College version of the IO course, "doing" and understanding influence is not even remotely part of the curriculum focus. All IO courses largely focus on planning expertise and staff functions. This is the military version of teaching architects only how to draw and to schedule sub-contractors for work but never teaching them about the house they are going to build.

IO Planners must be taught to become IO "doers". IRCs must be owned and at the disposal of commanders. The "mother may I" aspect of asking rather than tasking renders nearly every single so-called campaign at the mercy of those sitting all too often far away. To make matters worse, with limited tools available, just asking doesn't mean getting. This would never happen to an Infantry brigade where the commander has control of their resources and can maneuver with resources under their control.

Finally, on the topic of "IO Planning", DoD must build, train and deploy teams that represent all IRCs and that have control of the requisite resources. Every single member of these teams, much like SOF (Special Operations Forces ODAs (Operational Team Alphas) would have practitioner skills in addition to planning skills while cross-training on the skills of their teammates.

As it applies to this CD, this issue of tradecraft, or how we go about influence either overtly or in a covert manner, the **skills are best described as "lost to history"**. The last time we employed such tradecraft in scale was during the Cold War. A tiny fraction either inside or outside of DoD actually teach the skills now and in fact, are not taught at all by any doctrinal discipline. Having knowledge is one thing but that knowledge is irrelevant without use.

The predecessor to the CIA, the OSS had a structured approach to influence in support of the WWII war effort, which both taught and employed tradecraft. The OSS's Office of Morale, or MO for short was a largely successful enterprise. Follow-on efforts by the CIA continued but post the Cold War, for a long list of reasons, the efforts diminished substantially. For reasons of classification, we'll just leave this as described as "not up to the old standards and scale".

DoD, rarely delved into this arena post-Cold War and even then, on a very limited basis. Today, the efforts can be found only in niche areas and again, as with the IC, not at all on a scale that will make an impact strategically. The bottom line is that there is a critical gap of tradecraft that must be part and parcel of any effort to restore US influence capabilities.

5CD: failure to campaign:

The DoD definition of "campaign" is: "A series of related operations aimed at achieving strategic and operational objectives within a given time and space"

My single biggest frustration with DoD when it comes to influence is their failure to campaign. Once again, looking at my definition for influence: *"influence is achieved by a complex and intricate choreography of sustained actions, words and related activities wrapped around a core narrative that continually modifies behavior in a manner supportive of natsec objectives"* we can see that large or supporting influence campaigns, like their kinetic brothers require multiple things occurring in synch and often simultaneously. On a daily basis with few exceptions, this does not occur within DoD. CENTCOM being the exception and largely because they have received the lions' share of resources over the past few decades due to actually being involved in "shooting wars". Urgency is always good for innovation and being proactive.

All too often, much of DoD in their respective AOs, areas of operation, have little or nothing going on in the IO realm. They may have some military operation ongoing but there is a paltry amount of effort that amplifies and exploits the activity. PSYOP campaigns as a rule take months to put together. In our modern world, events come fast and furious and there is virtually no method to participate in real-time for nearly all units/ commands.

As that influence is dimensional thinking and most military planning is linear in nature, sometimes an example works better to illustrate a point.

Let's try a simple example using INDOPACOM as an example. In the example that follows, we'll look at the broad-brush focus of INDOPACOM and see what it would look like if they were doing multiple things simultaneously.

Before beginning, I want to make it clear that I'm not singling out INDOPACOM and that they are merely an example. In fact, the overworked and understaffed professionals responsible for the efforts do their best with what they have and a DoD bureaucracy that weighs them down in administrivia.

Per a statement from the SECDEF (Secretary of Defense) last June, this is the broad-brush focus of the command:

- **Preparedness** – Achieving peace through strength and employing effective deterrence requires a Joint Force that is prepared to win any conflict from its onset. The Department, alongside our Allies and partners, will ensure our combat-credible forces are forward-postured in the region. Furthermore, the Joint Force will prioritize investments that ensure lethality against high-end adversaries.

- **Partnerships** – Our unique network of Allies and partners is a force multiplier to achieve peace, deterrence, and interoperable warfighting capability. The Department is reinforcing its commitment to established Alliances and Partnerships, while also expanding and deepening relationships with new partners who share our respect for sovereignty, fair and reciprocal trade, and the rule of law.

- **Promotion of a Networked Region** – The Department is strengthening and evolving U.S. Alliances and Partnerships into a networked security architecture to uphold the international rules-based order. The Department also continues to cultivate intra-Asian security relationships capable of deterring aggression, maintaining stability, and ensuring free access to common domains.

Currently DoD focuses almost exclusively on big, demonstrable force-posturing to message their intent, occasionally highlighted but not amplified press releases of key leader engagements and exercises. There is very little PSYOP activity outside of some CT efforts and not in a focus region relatable to the points above. On a case by case basis use of other IRCs can be seen. Public Affairs doesn't fall under the IO effort and so is somewhat disjointed from the command's NSS efforts.

On any given day, the USG in some fashion is involved all over the INDOPACOM region, whether it be DOS, DoD or the myriad of other USG entities that engage with regional nations. **Every J39, the GCC individual in charge of IO should have every day, a spreadsheet in front of them that shows multiple activities by different IRCs executing their strategy in a multitude of locations if we are to start competing.**

The command's tasking as seen in the 3 bullets from the SECDEF are not mutually exclusive. Multiple IRCs and engagement with other USG entities doing something on behalf of the USG and the noted objectives could be doing something nearly every day to promote those objectives. This harkens back to our discussion earlier about narrative.

Here are just a few suggestions to make the point of campaigning rather than over-staffing individual events and efforts:

- Just doing FONs (Freedom of Navigation Ops) sends a message to our adversaries' military structure but does almost nothing for the other regional audiences. A **persistently employed** supporting narrative would explain to all relative audiences via print, SM (social media), TV and personal engagement the meaning of those FONs.

- **Aggressive engagement with narrative-centric messages** about a FON op across the region would fortify the belief of nations at risk of Chinese dominance that the US is a reliable security partner.

- Narrative-centric and aggressive messaging about a prominent commercial agreement between the US or a US corporation across the region demonstrates that the US is investing for the long term.

- Narrative-centric <u>PSYOP and CA, Civil Affairs team campaigns</u> to reach a variety of target audiences in the region that are critical to the overall US strategy and that are fully or partially isolated from regular media.

For centuries, Civil Affairs (CA) has long been called upon to facilitate stable and secure transitions from military to civilian control and from conflict to peace. Recently, CA is helping to bring together whole-of-nation elements to engage partners and mitigate conflict. In short, CA is a major national strategic capability that helps end and prevent wars. This capability along with Military Information Support (formerly Psychological Operations) and Foreign Area Officers, comprises the only part of the Joint Force specifically suited for Peace & Stability Operations as well as Engagement.

-Holshek 2015

- The US, especially via SOF, trains militaries around the world and all over the INDOPACOM region but we rarely are told the bigger picture of "why", just that they did it for security cooperation. This isn't enough, PSYOP, PA and outreach to the media needs to show that security cooperation is the US's way of investing in and looking towards a long future relationship. Again, this is the whole point of narrative, to give meaning to what audiences see, read, hear or otherwise.

- The old adage about how long it takes to build trust is relevant here. Building trust, not just with foreign militaries or through diplomatic channels is not enough. Popular understanding by local audiences of reliability must be built as well. In some cases, this is even more important than high-profile diplomatic efforts because local politicians/ leaders need to fully and accurately understand our intent as well.

The bottom line to this handful of suggestions is that **robust influence campaigns are virtually absent from DoD operations**.

For those that are still struggling to get the point, here's another analogy. Now that we are in election season, we are bombarded with ads, appearances, personal engagement, canvassers knocking on doors, flyers, tweets and so on. These happen all day/ every day. If you don't campaign the risk is losing your audience to a competitor. China follows the US campaign model meticulously. There is no event, idea or otherwise that they don't use every tool or IRC in their toolbox to influence. We are literally "bringing a knife to a gunfight". **We're not just overmatched by resources but willingness to compete.**

Summary

As this long white paper edges towards its conclusion, a gentle reminder seems appropriate regarding my opening comments. This stark assessment and discussion of the inability to influence in support of our NSS objectives has been a labor of love, albeit, "tough love". It's never easy to lay heavy criticism on colleagues and the profession that you have a passion for, no matter how well-informed. Still, there is too much at stake to not speak truth to power.

At some point we have to be honest with ourselves that exclusively building big ticket defense tools such as planes, ships and tanks are not enough to keep us safe and relevant on the world stage. We're being challenged and beaten at every turn in the one primary area demonstrably the most important and based on our highest national security documents... influence.

Senior leadership over the past couple of decades has relatively ignored the obvious or been unwilling to address the critical vulnerability of having no effective influence architecture. As we can see from our primary threats such as Russia, China, Iran, N. Korea, extremists etc. we're losing ground. The reason we're losing ground is because we've either forgotten or ignored something that we were not only good at, but were good at leading others with... influence.

Our complacency and yes, some arrogance that as a unipolar power for the last two decades was the only influence, we needed has put us far behind the power curve and at a time when we can least afford it. Now, not tomorrow is the time to change direction and correct our mistakes.

The issues and critical deficiencies discussed here are the minimum, "must dos" to change course but they are merely band aids meant to stop the bleeding in our current losses. A complete overhaul across the spectrum of the USG is the ultimate goal for serious professionals that focus on facts, not stove-piped visions.

In order to regain our former prowess, we must start from the ground up and train professional influencers and employ them in teams that include the specialists of the many disciplines and who have access to the tools and resources required. This isn't just an IC or DoD thing. These teams, belonging to an influence organisation must be from across the spectrum of the USG. That organization must have tasking authority and be time responsive in order to operate in the moment, next month and for the long-term.

In order for influence professionals to be on target, we need to develop whole new training methodologies and curriculums and that includes a special addition of intelligence professionals that meet the unique collection, analysis and assessment needs of the influence community.

With the legal complexities, there must also be a legal team that focuses on the ethical but not risk-averse campaigning required to influence successfully. Protecting our rights and protecting the nation are not mutually exclusive.

I reemphasize that this paper merely scratches the surface but it's a start and the minimum requirement for our current security needs. We can do this. While the reformation will be hard, it's still far easier than putting a man on the moon or curing polio and other diseases. It only requires the courage to do so and historically, this is something that isn't in short supply for our nation. It only needs to be woken up.

Conclusion

This white paper has been put off for years too long and I accept that responsibility. Our national security environment now, more than at any time in modern US history is not up to its challenges. To be blunt, we're living out the old saying in the natsec community of "planning for the last war". Frankly, we're not even up to our current ones. This is not from a lack of resources and talent but the inability to acknowledge our true deficits and act decisively on the knowledge.

As we go down the road of attempting to effectively pursue our national security strategy, we're traveling with blinders on and married to risk averse and antiquated thinking. I personally believe that this is because it's just too hard to acknowledge the truth of the changes demanded by our threats. We can do as we did just prior to WWI or WWII and put our head in the sand and wait to adapt after it's too late or… we can use our knowledge and prepare and execute intelligently. Failing to prepare for the challenge at hand has historically cost us dearly. I personally am not a fan of that option, so at risk of angering many in my profession, this paper was dedicated to "speaking truth to power".

Every one of our stated natsec challenges is influence-centric. Strategists and reputable think tanks have been saying this now for a decade or so. Of course, the terms they often have used are like, "hybrid warfare", "conflict in the grey zone" or operations beneath the threshold of war. In the natsec community it would seem as if there is an allergic reaction to using the word influence but I'm old school and prefer to get to the bottom line. **We are in an era where influence is the battlefield, not terrain**.

The contents of this paper, even at 20 plus pages barely scratches the surface of deficiencies, opportunities and analysis required to bring the natsec community up to speed. As you can see from the linked websites, manuals, policy papers etc. a full review and set of recommendations would well exceed 1000 pages. Though this topic is deserving of that number of pages, our threats are far too severe to not act on the bare minimum deficiencies articulated here.

In order to achieve a modicum of proficiency in the deficiencies discussed, change must become the objective of every senior member of the relevant agencies and entities. It will take courage, political capital and persistence, but for those who hold their oaths of office and/ or service sacred, the requisite changes are your obligation, not your choice.

*We have entered the age of mass customization of messaging, narrative, and persuasion. We need a strategy to counter Russian, as well as others, information operations and prepare the United States organizationally for long-term IO competition with a constantly changing set of adversaries large and small. It is said that where there is a will, there is a way. At this point, ways are available. **The question is, do we have the will to use them?***

-Waltzman 2017

I am not suggesting that my thoughts are exclusively "right" and am always open to input from well informed challengers. If you disagree, please do so and let's elevate the discussion of innovation to those with the power to change things. In fact, I would be so bold as to suggest that principle leaders take a week together (virtually, in wake of the COVID 19 crisis) and hammer out a way forward on at least the handful of critical deficiencies discussed here. That meeting needs to have proactive outcomes that put the changes to work immediately if not sooner. Our adversaries are light years ahead. We don't have time for those entities involved to get bogged down in the USG bureaucratic norm of "paralysis by analysis".

Finally, thank you to the colleagues and other professionals who have worked tirelessly to lead and mentor me throughout my career. I have no doubt that those mentors will well receive this "tough love" because they planted the seeds long ago. This may be my voice on these pages but it speaks for the very best and brightest in our field and I suspect, also for the overwhelming majority of others.

Godspeed to those senior leaders who will take up the challenge of this desperately needed natsec reform and I'll leave you this final quote:

If not now, when? If not you, who?

-Hillel the Elder

1st Century Rabbinic scholar

Brainwashing: An Extremist Influence Strategy

Happy Monday to TAT readers,

Well, it's Monday, so let's get the hard stuff out of the way first. I woke up on a mission to help people understand, the insanity that has gripped our nation in the Trump era. What has prompted today's article is that Saturday, I posted a very short, factually precise truth about today's GOP. As followers know by now, I don't support any party, choosing to adopt the traditions and heed the warnings of our first POTUS, George Washington. From my perspective, they do not support the ideals ensconced in our founding documents. Today's

GOP, brainwashed by professional influencers, makes Washington's threat advisory from his Farewell Address in 1796, all too terrifying.

Background

As I noted pre-emptively on Saturday's post, I would lose several subscribers by telling the truth about today's version of the GOP. I lost 9 and I haven't the slightest regret. I write to express truth that matters on issues of acute national security threats, not to acquire subscribers. The **insider threat** to our nation did not disappear when Trump left office or for that matter, after indictments for 91 felonies. The conversion of the once proud GOP into an extremist movement did not happen overnight, nor expressly with Trump. **The premise of today's article is, "if we don't see the threat accurately, we cannot protect ourselves."**

This has everything to do with my expertise in **Narrative Warfare**. It has nothing to do with my political beliefs. If you see today's article as political in nature, it may have more to do with your own political identity, rather than the acute threat that MAGA is to our nation. For a fuller understanding of Narrative Warfare and today's Republican Party, I include the following link to my "*Lincoln Project*" podcast interview, just prior to the 2022 election.

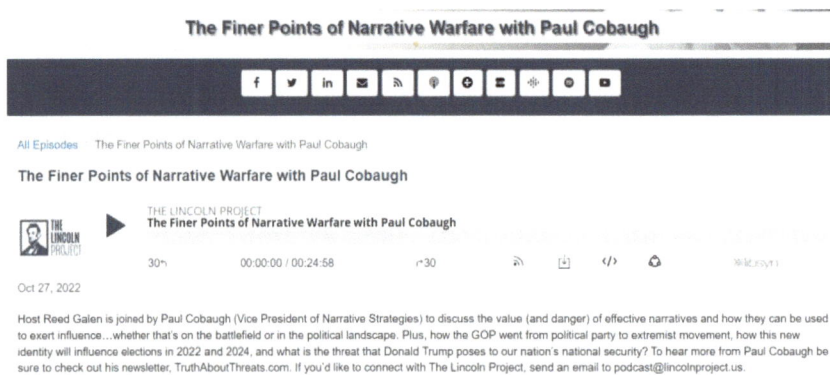

Screenshot from the Lincoln Project podcast.

What makes today's GOP so dangerous to American democracy is not that they are Republicans but that they have been, in 1960's terms, "brainwashed." Although I am not necessarily a fan of the term, "brainwashed," **I use it in order for many readers to better understand the points I am making. In other words, the un-American ideology of MAGA triggers them subconsciously and that they have little to no power to resist these triggers. This is actually how "narrative works."** There are plenty of professional terms floating around this phenomenon, but narrative is actually what is occurring. The most succinct explanation of narrative is: **"it is how human beings make meaning out of everything they experience, based on their own, specific identity."** Our identities evolve over the course of our lifetime which means that they can be shaped by a wide variety of factors. Propaganda is one method, albeit it a long process. This is the route that FOX news took. This applies to group identities, as well as individuals.

For example, most of America loves football but… we become rabidly tribal regarding different teams vs. our team. The **identities** of Cleveland Brown fans (yes, I am a long-suffering Browns fan) are similar in terms of loyalty but share very little in common with Cincinnati Bengal fans, even though they are in the same small state of Ohio. Marketing Cleveland Browns products based on their specific identity traits would be a success, everywhere but in Southwestern Ohio, in the Cincinnati area. Tribalizing is powerful when it comes to defending the tribe. **If this sounds a lot like US politics, it is because it is precisely the same.**

brainwashing noun

brain·wash·ing (ˈbrān-ˌwȯ-shiŋ ◄») -ˌwä-

Synonyms of *brainwashing* >

1 : a forcible indoctrination to induce someone to give up basic political, social, or religious beliefs and attitudes and to accept contrasting regimented ideas

2 : persuasion by propaganda or salesmanship

brainwash (ˈbrān-ˌwȯsh ◄») -ˌwäsh *transitive verb*

brainwash noun

brainwasher noun

In **NW/ Narrative Warfare**, identity is the key and those who understand how to analyze specific identities have the upper hand. To date, there are very few of these specialists available to the US national security community. This is due to the entrenched but failed, defense contractor system and ridiculous Pentagon doctrine on such matters. I have written on this often and so won't lay it all out again. For those with interest though, this earlier TAT article and its embedded links will provide detailed insight into our self-imposed risk.

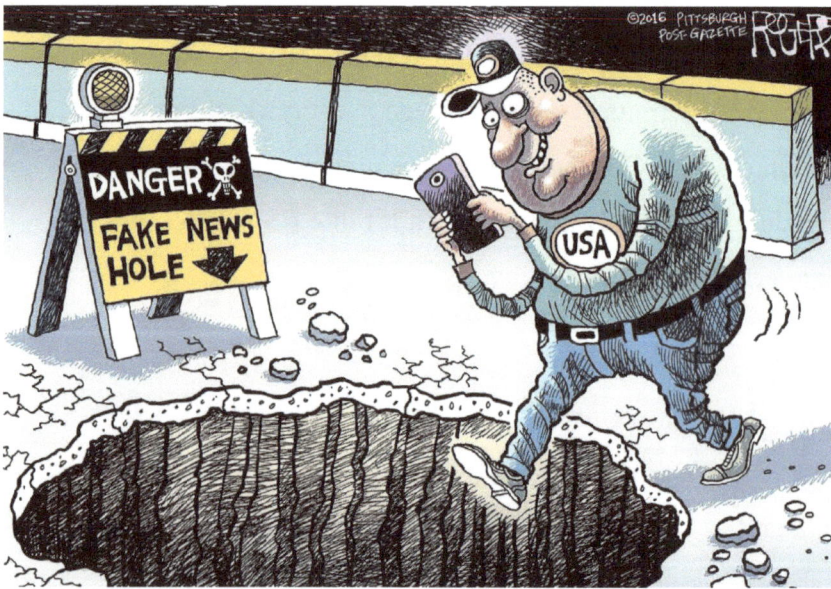

Protecting our nation from Mis and Disinformation, requires true expertise at Ethical Influence (truthaboutthreats.com)

There are only two ways to fully understand the identity of an audience: first is to know how to do the research and two, build it yourself over a long time. In this case, the principled conservatism of POTUS Eisenhower or H.W. Bush has over time and with the advent of FOX News, completely reshaped the specific identity of **the Republican Party. It is no longer remotely close to principled conservatism, but an extremist movement advocating for our enemies, advocating for unbridled Oligarchism and against the keystone of our republic, our Constitution.**

Fortunately, FOX and company don't understand identity. The problem is, they do understand audience conditioning. This simply means that instead of analyzing their audiences, the built a controllable identity over nearly thirty years of subversive programming.

Now that we understand the criticality of identity to predictable influence operations, let's move on to the threat imposed by having one of only two, major American political parties fully conditioned to MAGA ideology. **As a quick note regarding the use of the word, "conditioned," this is exactly the same as Pavlov's famous experiment involving a dog and a "conditioned response to a bell."**

As it pertains to the Republican Party and FOX News, three-word chants like, **lock her up**, **drain the swamp**, **stop the steal** etc., in conjunction with a color pattern, music, symbolism etc. are no different from Pavlov's bell. They trigger a conditioned response that is predictable. **This is how an entire political party, over the roughly 30 years of FOX has "conditioned" their audience to accept and tribally defend such un-American concepts as God, guns and Trump.** In fact, if you Google the phrase, *God, Guns and Trump*, you will be astounded at the pages of far-right websites that appear on your computer screen. This is conditioning, brainwashing, propaganda and all together, Narrative Warfare against our Republic, by people brainwashed to predictably act on their subconscious impulses. **Expecting these folks to act rationally is little different than asking the sun to rise in the West tomorrow morning. They have almost no control of these impulses.**

Before conditioning

FOOD   **SALIVATION**
(UCS)   **(UCR)**

BELL   **NO RESPONSE**

ding dong

During conditioning

BELL +   **SALIVATION**
FOOD   **(UCR)**
(UCS)

ding dong
+

After conditioning

BELL   **SALIVATION**
(CS)   **(CR)**

ding dong

The MAGA movement has made brainwashed sheep of once principled conservatives. They will say and do, exactly as conditioned to, by professional influencers.

As it pertains to next year's Presidential election, there is simply no reason to expect anything different from voters who vote Republican based on their identity. Once established, it is a very hard sell to undo such conditioning as described above. Like a river cutting through a mountain over a millennium or so, it requires years, sometimes generations to alter an established identity in a group. We see this all across America with different ethnic communities sustaining traditions harkening back to native homelands. Yes, they're all Americans but there is still, nation of origin identity traits. Kilts, Mariachi music, lederhosen, Feng Shui, hula, high tea etc. are just some minor examples of different identity traits that endure. Sure, all can be American by citizenship but generations' old traits, are still part and parcel of the overall identity of most citizens.

So, what do we do about this threat from an intentionally curated identity for the MAGA folks? First, never ask the US national security community for help because they just don't know how to address this threat and refuse to learn. We will have to do this ourselves, by actually engaging privately and publicly on what our national identity entails, not the fake patriotism of

113

MAGA. This is called a narrator, audience relationship. Everyone can be a narrator and throughout our lives, we all do advocate for ourselves, based on our needs and how our identity perceives those needs.

So that DHS and the FBI understand, my frustration with their failure regarding adversarial influencers like Russia, global far-right movements etc. is more due to their unwillingness to learn and execute a modern strategy. The same applies to the Pentagon and IC/ Intelligence Communities. Washington is overflowing with alleged experts, and most are the same that have failed us for forty years plus. Also, as evidenced by GOP Congressmen raising hell with DHS regarding their plans for a disinformation board, our nation is defenseless again foreign and domestic influencers.

As that I have lived and professionally spent most of my uniformed career in the field of influence, I have seen the devastating effects stemming from our persistent failures in this field. We failed at stemming Islamic Narrative Warfare and we now have failed with a far more sinister, domestic threat coming from our own, voting citizens. Sure, all across the Beltway and beyond, the national security community at large is holding countless, expensive conferences, authorizing case studies and giving away our tax dollars to those with a record of failure, not success. This will not save us during next year's election season.

We nearly lost our republic to those brainwashed GOP voters and their violent extremist mobs of January 6th, 2021. In the meantime, nothing of substance has been done to counteract the global far-right movement, that shares ideology with today's Republican party. Due to Svengali-like media along the lines of FOX, NewsMax, OAN and the myriad of other websites calling themselves news but actually, propaganda sites for far-right ideology, the number of Republican voters who voted for Trump or trumpish candidates in 2016, grew in number by 2020 and there will almost certainly be more, in 2024. To those in my field, this was predictable but to our national security community and the army of election pollsters, there was and still is shock.

Now I may not be the sharpest knife in the drawer, but I know my field well. Our Think/ Do Tank, Narrative Strategies, is the cutting-edge organization that understands this field. There are no surprises to us, just fear over what another far-right administration will do to our nation.

DHS somehow believes that there is only a CYBER answer to this threat. How foolish! Influence is a human endeavor and machines, as of now cannot understand how humans make meaning. Most researchers in the CYBER realm are going down rabbit holes with considering that they are on paths that cannot produce success. The FBI, the same. As noted earlier, Republican congressmen bar DHS from even trying to outline the parameters of the propaganda used against our nation. Even if there were a "disinformation board," fact-checking does not work in combatting false, established narratives. Only better narratives, professionally constructed and managed over time, can make a difference.

THE NEVER-ENDING RACE

As I said before and will say until no one will listen, **American citizens will have to right the USS America, by ourselves**. A toxic political landscape where parties compete for identities, leaves us hopelessly paralyzed in hyper-partisanship. The right is mired in far-right, embedded extremism and the left is still talking about policy, instead of like President Biden, fighting "for the soul of our nation." POTUS is spot on, but where the heck is the rest of the team? Like I said, I will not advocate for any party, but I will sure as hell work against the GOP who is incapable of shedding their extremist, curated political identity.

The whole point of today's TAT is to present the problem as succinctly as possible. To recap, our problem is that today's Republican Party is fully committed to the un-American narrative of the far-right. Their identity will continue to produce the same results until someone does something about it. There is nothing our defense community can do about it with their current tools and understanding. This puts American democracy at severe risk of being converted into a White, Christian Nationalist nation run by authoritarians and oligarchs. It is precisely that simple. Trump very nearly accomplished this in one term. With his base intact, nothing being done about the influencers who peddle far-right/ GOP propaganda, he or someone like him will succeed in another term.

If you don't believe me… look who is really running the House of Representatives. There isn't one single principled conservative among them. If there were, they would be raising so much hell that you could hear it in your sleep. **If pollsters and the US national security community don't get serious about this threat, they will be out of a job. Not because they are not good, committed citizens but because… there will be no more American democracy.**

In the end, we should have heeded Washington's warning in his Farewell address. We haven't and his vision for an America dominated by parties or "factions" in colonial terms, has come to pass.

I will conclude today's article with the following introduction to Washington's Farewell Address, regarding factions. They are ominous.

INTRODUCTION

Prepared by the United States Senate Historical Office

In September 1796, worn out by burdens of the presidency and attacks of political foes, George Washington announced his decision not to seek a third term. With the assistance of Alexander Hamilton and James Madison, Washington composed in a "Farewell Address" his political testament to the nation. Designed to inspire and guide future generations, the address also set forth Washington's defense of his administration's record and embodied a classic statement of Federalist doctrine.

Washington's principal concern was for the safety of the eight-year-old Constitution. He believed that the stability of the Republic was threatened by the forces of geographical sectionalism, political factionalism, and interference by foreign powers in the nation's domestic affairs. He urged Americans to subordinate sectional jealousies to common national interests. Writing at a time before political parties had become accepted as vital extraconstitutional, opinion-focusing agencies, Washington feared that they carried the seeds of the nation's destruction through petty factionalism. Although Washington was in no sense the father of American isolationism, since he recognized the necessity of temporary associations for "extraordinary emergencies," he did counsel against the establishment of "permanent alliances with other countries," connections that he warned would inevitably be subversive of America's national interest.

Washington did not publicly deliver his Farewell Address. It first appeared on September 19, 1796, in the Philadelphia *Daily American Advertiser* and then in papers around the country.

In January 1862, with the Constitution endangered by civil war, a thousand citizens of Philadelphia petitioned Congress to commemorate the forthcoming 130th anniversary of George Washington's birth by providing that "the Farewell Address of Washington be read aloud on the morning of that day in one or the other of the Houses of Congress." Both houses agreed and assembled in the House of Representatives' chamber on February 22, 1862, where Secretary of the Senate John W. Forney "rendered 'The Farewell Address' very effectively," as one observer recalled.

The practice of reading the Farewell Address did not immediately become a tradition. The address was first read in regular legislative sessions of the Senate in 1888 and the House in 1899. (The House continued the practice until 1984.) Since 1893 the Senate has observed Washington's birthday by selecting one of its members to read the Farewell Address. The assignment alternates between members of each political party. At the conclusion of each reading, the appointed senator inscribes his or her name and brief remarks in a black, leather-bound book maintained by the secretary of the Senate.

The version of the address printed here is taken from the original of the final manuscript in the New York Public Library provided courtesy of The Papers of George Washington. The only changes have been to modernize spelling, capitalization, and punctuation.

Screenshot from the introduction to Washington's Farewell Address, read every year on the Senate floor.

The alternate domination of one faction over another, sharpened by the spirit of revenge natural to party dissension, which in different ages and countries has perpetrated the most horrid enormities, is itself a frightful despotism. But this leads at length to a more formal and permanent despotism. The disorders and miseries which result gradually incline the minds of men to seek security and repose in the absolute power of an individual; and sooner or later the chief of some prevailing faction, more able or more fortunate than his competitors, turns this disposition to the purposes of his own elevation on the ruins of public liberty.

- President George Washington
- Farewell Address
- September 19, 1796

There is an opinion that parties in free countries are useful checks upon the administration of the government and serve to keep alive the spirit of liberty. This within certain limits is probably true—and in governments of a monarchical cast patriotism may look with indulgence, if not with favor, upon the spirit of party. But in those of the popular character, in governments purely elective, it is a spirit not to be encouraged. From their natural tendency, it is certain there will always be enough of that spirit for every salutary purpose. And there being constant danger of excess, the effort ought to be by force of public opinion to mitigate and assuage it. A fire not to be quenched, it demands a uniform vigilance to prevent its bursting into a flame, lest instead of warming it should consume.

- President George Washington
- Farewell Address
- September 19, 1796

*They serve to organize faction; to give it an artificial and extraordinary force;
to put in the place of the delegated will of the nation the will of a party, often
a small but artful and enterprising minority of the community; and, according
to the alternate triumphs of different parties, to make the public
administration the mirror of the ill concerted and incongruous projects of
faction, rather than the organ of consistent and wholesome plans digested by
common councils and modified by mutual interests. However, combinations or
associations of the above description may now and then answer popular ends,
they are likely, in the course of time and things, to become potent engines by
which cunning, ambitious, and unprincipled men will be enabled to subvert
the power of the people and to usurp for themselves the reins of government,
destroying afterwards the very engines which have lifted them to unjust
dominion.*

- President George Washington
- Farewell Address
- September 19, 1796

Modern-Day Minutemen and Women

Chapter 4, published in July of 2019 is the beginning of the quest to rally the troops, or more clearly, US voters to the cause of defending our next Presidential election. In the 3 three previous years, the inform and educate voters effort regarding election security by the US IC, and private entities exhausted itself. Like almost every aspect of our lives these days, the efforts were cast as political points of view which alienated at least, 1/3 of US voters. The normal response to a rallying cry by the alienated faction was something along the line of; "fake news", Russian didn't attack us" which evolved to, "if they did, it didn't matter".

In these same 3 plus years, the IC and Pentagon made very little progress in election security outside the realm of select CYBER aspects. Now, in our last, pre-election year, the only answer to the malign influence was to rally those willing to become "Modern-Day Minutemen" and train them for defense. To complicate matters more, it now is not only Russia, but China, Iran and other adversarial State and non-state actors lobbing salvos of mis/ disinformation over the parapets of the US election.

The chapter 4 article is literally a short history lesson and a rallying cry to Patriots.

Homeland Security Today Magazine: Everyone Must Be a Modern-Day Minuteman to Protect Our Election

July 31, 2019

As dawn broke, crisp and clear on the 19th of April 1775, 77 patriots urgently formed themselves into a skirmish line on the Lexington Commons. Their formation looked much like they had practiced once a month for the past year or so. As they peered through the dawn light at the 700 professional British troops at the other end of the commons, it was clear that this was going to be no practice. Within minutes of first being alerted, there they stood, preparing for the first time to offer armed resistance against the battle-hardened troops who'd fought all across the British empire. These intrepid souls, known as "Minutemen," as dictated by law a year earlier had been formed from a mix of local militias, in which membership was a requirement. They were a cross-section of early colonial life, part native, part immigrant, and from differing backgrounds. These men may have assembled because of the legal requirement but what truly bound them together was their deep, burning passion to be free of the meddlesome oppression of a foreign government.

When shots cut the cool, crisp dawn air, eight minutemen fell dead in what would become the first casualties of our war for independence. That first skirmish on the commons in Lexington led to the North Bridge and Concord shortly afterwards, where fate reversed its course for the British troops. All along their advance into Concord and throughout their retreat back to Boston, minutemen continued to pour out of their towns, villages and farms, until their numbers exceeded 3,000.

The brief dawn success in Lexington for the seven hundred British grenadiers and light infantry that had marched out from Boston was their last of the expedition. They would suffer 79 dead and 149 wounded by the time they limped back into Boston having been under assault the entire way. Colonial casualties would reach 49 killed and 39 wounded. Britain would be stunned and humiliated by their encounter with the patriots, which signaled full rebellion. Eight years later, the humiliation complete, Britain would recognize our independence. American resolve in the face of a threat would never again be underestimated.

The relevance of minutemen to this article is that it was organized citizens in 1775 with little formal training but an ironclad loyalty to their community and common values who answered the call to resist a foreign attack. In our past two election cycles we have been attacked by a foreign enemy and it will be up to modern-day minutemen to answer the call to protect our free and fair elections.

We as a nation are still unprepared as we wade deeply into our next election cycle. In the absence of an effective, wide-spectrum strategy by the U.S. government to secure our elections, it will depend on all Americans to fill the gaps in our defenses. The weapons of our modern minutemen, though, are not muskets and sabers but fact-checkers, credible sources of information, and the ability (and willingness) to discuss issues rather than fight our fellow citizens. Digital and media literacy and, most of all, at a moment's notice, being willing to engage the enemy in protection of our values is of the utmost importance. The most important weapon, bar none, is still courage. **The courage to speak and act on the whole truth, regardless of tribal political affiliations.**

It's quite simple: If we don't defend our Presidential election from the ramparts of truth, we don't defend it at all. There are countless courageous, trained professionals working within the national security community but they can only do so much. DHS and their national security partners are working on election infrastructure, cybersecurity, etc., but that still will not be enough. **Foreign enemies influencing voters with propaganda, dis- and mis-information is a vulnerable unattended gap in our defenses that only everyday citizens can fill.** This is precisely the one area in which every American has a chance to stand shoulder-to-shoulder with other patriotic citizens of all beliefs to ensure that it is truly voters, not Mr. Putin or his like, that make our decisions at the ballot box.

In our upcoming Presidential election, every citizen, regardless of political belief, has the opportunity and responsibility to take on the mantle of "minuteman" (or woman) to collectively defend our birthright of freedom – especially that of free and fair elections – from attack by hostile foreign enemies.

Introduction

Last year, I had the honor of becoming affiliated with Homeland Security Today Magazine as a contributor when they published my white paper *A Five-Point Strategy to Oppose Russian Narrative Warfare.* The reason for this current article is simple; to date, the U.S. government, outside of a few areas of concern, is still quite far from enacting a comprehensive and executable strategy for protecting our upcoming 2020 election. Sadly, we are still vulnerable. This begs the question: Who at this late date can help and where should they focus their attention? The DHS and others in the national security community are doing what they can but are hobbled by bureaucracy, regulation and unaddressed bills in the Senate. The most vulnerable aspect of foreign influence targeting voters is something virtually unaddressed by any U.S. government strategy. This leaves us, the citizenry, to address what we can. In a "good news/ bad news" sort of way, the good news is that one of our most dangerous vulnerabilities is something the average citizen can contribute to the most.

The following article regarding the role that every citizen can play is relatively short compared to last years' white paper. It is also relatively blunt. My apologies up front if it is too blunt for many readers. Time is short before the 2024 Presidential election and there is no time to dally around with subtle niceties. Adversaries like Russia, China and Iran, with Russia being the most serious threat, can and will continue to interfere with our national birthright, ours. The wolf – or, rather, the Russian bear – is literally at our door.

The following article is actually one of the five strategy points in last year's article and was entitled *Resilience*. To be more specific, it is actually **"narrative resilience" (NR)**, which simply put is the war over the meaning of information, not war over information. The very reason I placed resilience as the first of the five points last year is precisely why I am discussing it here again. Citizens are the primary targets of foreign influence simply because, as targets of influence go, we are the most vulnerable. This, of course, means left/right, Republican/Democrat, liberal/conservative or any other political beliefs must work together. After all, our first duty is to the nation, not a political party.

There are several links embedded to either support my points or to provide valuable resources to the readers.

BLUF:

1. The 2020 U.S. election is hurtling toward us.
2. The U.S. IC (intelligence community) has unequivocally concluded that Russia attempted to influence the 2016 and 2018 U.S. elections and will continue to do so with the 2020 elections.
3. We, as in the U.S. government, are still woefully unprepared to fend off significant and ongoing foreign influence attacks from the likes of Russia, China, and Iran, etc.
4. One of our most vulnerable areas is that U.S. citizens are still allowing themselves to be victimized by enemy narratives by way of mis/disinformation or, as commonly called, "fake news."
5. With far too few national defense tools, processes and oversight, the average U.S. citizen will need to provide much of the supporting effort by becoming "Minutemen" of sorts against foreign influence attacks.

6. The most commonly accepted name for this is "resilience," but in fact it is "narrative resilience."

The reason that NR is so important is simply because "hardening" our personal defenses as citizens against influence is the core of the issue. In military parlance, a "hardened target" is difficult to penetrate. By default, if mis/disinformation doesn't penetrate, their effects are, by default, mitigated. A cornerstone of Russian influence operations is false and misleading information disseminated through various channels. Russian propaganda sustained their narratives, which focused on dividing U.S. society along well-establish fault lines. In fact, their agenda was to make these fault lines far worse and more divisive than actually exist.

The most common channels in 2016, 2018 and to the present are social media. Russia's intent is to deceive, divide and erode collective adversarial resistance to their aggression. As their targets are primarily civilian audiences, it becomes essential to "harden civilian targets" to the effects of such activity. NR is, in fact, the process of hardening these targets. First and foremost, this requires educating audiences and divorcing them from "identity politics" or adversarial narratives that are so influential in exploiting such politics.

As an analogy it's helpful to look at NR much the same as taking protective measures against infection by a communicable disease. Washing hands, avoiding infected people and places or employing all manner of protective measures contribute to NR and cumulatively mitigate and manage the risk of infection and exposure. Malign influence, such as has been and is currently and aggressively employed by Russia, has no absolute cure, hence minimizing the risk is a critical, pragmatic and largely achievable option. We cannot completely cure ourselves of Russian or other influence, but we absolutely can minimize it to the point that it's not an overt threat.

Building NR in a political landscape as divisive as we currently have in the U.S. is difficult but not unattainable. In order to do so, we must return to our collective values and resist Russian narratives that exploit our differences. This means that we need narrators from top to bottom who focus our attention around our collective values rather than those that emotionally trigger division. As an indicator of just how important this is, we can only look at how many resources Russia applies to promoting and exploiting divisive topics. Their thinking on this is sound: A divided democracy is an impotent democracy. If it were not important, they would spend their time and resources elsewhere.

The question regarding NR is mostly centered on "how to mentor citizens to resist emotionally triggering narratives filled with divisive content that is inaccurate and harmful." Recent efforts by some of the Nordic countries have employed some novel and very helpful tactics to "inoculate" voters against Russian narrative warfare. Their focus has been to require opposing political parties to commit to educating and mentoring all voters, not just those politically aligned, to recognize, report and expose media focused on malign influence by Russia. Finland, in particular, has a remarkable program in their public schools that teaches critical thinking and how to sort out what is fake or misleading. NR is everyone's responsibility. In fact, it's the one area in which competing political partisans could and should agree. Neither side should wish to win an election if a hostile foreign power lends aid to their side. This is, frankly, un-American.

Resiliency recommendations against Russian malign influence:

Elections free of dishonest content, especially that which is inserted by hostile foreign powers, requires more than lip service by leadership from both sides of the political divide. It also requires resources. Faith in national institutions such as law enforcement, the intelligence community and the military are non-negotiables, as well. Voters go where leaders follow and thus it becomes a requirement for leadership to drive these requirements, as in "lead by example."

Narrative is a primary component of hardening the target

Though often misunderstood, narrative is the way humans make sense of the world around them. In its simplest form, it's a story that gives meaning to myriad words, actions, etc., that people are exposed to. Every person, family, tribe, city, state, region or country has their own unique narrative about "who they are." What Russia employs against us is "Narrative Warfare." In other words, it's not a war over information but a war over the meaning of information. Bad actors such as Russian trolls and those who tweet, retweet or post dishonest content use that content to trigger responses in their audiences. What this does actually is "trigger" our unique and group identities or, specifically, our "narrative identities." These specific identities have existed for generations and will in some form for generations to come. If we don't learn to deal with how we are triggered now, the vulnerabilities will always exist and be a threat.

To the point as how narrative matters to protecting our nation, it is simply that we all, right/left, Republican or Democrat, etc., share more common elements of national identity than we all believe. If we recognize that we share an identity through a common narrative then, by default, we must band together to resist anything that will harm our identity. Many times, this is interpreted as "tribal politics." Tribes formed to protect like individuals from outside enemies. Those with the strongest bonds of common identity do a far better job of protecting the "tribe." The American tribal identity includes all of us, not the lesser tribes that make up our nation. Hence, the resolute bonds of our national identity that served us so well in two world wars and other challenges still exists. If we bond over these bonds or, rather, our identity, we should have no problem keeping Mr. Putin at bay.

Russia and other influencers attempt to harmfully divide us along identity (tribal) lines. Race, ethnicity, social issues, etc., are examples of this. While we all have some sort of membership in lesser tribes, it's our national identity that should be primary. If we allow Russia or others to pit us against each other, they succeed and we fail. For the purpose of national security, all Americans who see themselves as patriotic have a responsibility to place national identity ahead of other types such as party, state, gender, race, ethnicity, etc.

"Hardening" a unified national identity by solidifying our core values by default reduces the threat of divisive narrative warfare. "Who we are as a nation" is based on our historical narrative. This identity, once hardened, reduces the threat from weaponized and divisive narratives from Russia and other aggressors. Again, identity is a critical component of narrative. Like the old adage regarding feuding siblings who will fight each other but band together to resist outside threats, the U.S. populace must do the same. **Our internal issues are for us to sort out without allowing outside threats to exploit our divisions. Like siblings, we can disagree fervently with each other but must band together to deny foreign malign actors "a say" in our domestic problems.**

U.S. political parties would have us believe that there are two primary identities and that they do not share common values. Though this is a common perception, it is far from the truth. Both political "sides" have a responsibility to establish this unified, though often at odds identity. Though there are differing opinions, sometimes dramatically, both sides still adhere to the common core values which revolve around our Constitutional principles.

Leaders who constantly pit one side against the other as "un-American" dangerously provide Russia with the opportunity to further exploit our differences for their own purposes. Intentionally pitting one side vs. the other is not only dangerous, it is un-American. Remember, divide and conquer is one of the oldest and most effective of military strategies. Why should we make Russia's job easier by allowing them to do so?

Education regarding digital literacy, though a much longer approach, is a critical element of NR. Students and all adults have the responsibility of citizenship to be accurately informed. One of our most trying problems with mis/disinformation is that it is easier to accept content that bolsters parts of our identity regardless if it is true, accurate and in context. Tragically, a large number of Americans now habitually believe that "winning for their political side" is more important than solving a problem for the entire nation. Remember, being a Republican or Democrat is a lesser, not a primary, identity!

The easiest way to trigger someone's identity is to share something that they wish to believe, based on their identity. Political parties are notorious for using this technique. Just because some bit of information suits your identity doesn't make it true. If you base your loyalty on dishonest content, you are not only cheating yourself but your fellow citizens. If this is the case, you are the problem, not the solution. In short: stop it! It's not only immoral but patently un-American. If the leaders you follow do so, either stop following or insist on an honest narrative from them as the price of loyalty.

Learning to fact-check, doing credible research and applying critical analysis are all hallmarks of a resilient populace. Education and mentoring regarding these three elements are the responsibility of schools, parents, community leaders, etc. Yes, every single citizen is either part of the problem or part of the solution. Curriculum and teaching techniques must be instituted in our schools and public institutions beginning at a very early grade level and be supported by parents and other respected community leaders. Facts, in context matter. My parents always said, "If you have to use dishonesty to win an argument, you should probably change your opinion."

Public and credible renunciation of false and misleading content by trusted leaders and institutions is a "must-do." Challenging all "fake news" or otherwise is required consistently, not only when it "helps" your political/social beliefs. I cannot emphasize this point enough. Leaders from the local level through the highest office have a citizen's responsibility regarding accurate, in-context information. Those who fail in this aspect of resiliency have no business in a leadership role. Those who accept dishonesty on face value without doing their homework have consciously abdicated their responsibility as a citizen.

Conclusion

This short piece merely discusses the most essential basics of **narrative resiliency.** The topic is easily deserving of an entire book. We don't have time either to write or have every American voter read such a book with our elections bearing down on us. There is also no magic solution that government can provide. This piece of our national defense falls under the title of "responsible citizenship." With the few simple tips listed below, every citizen can increase their NR immeasurably.

An untrained and unaware citizenry is exceptionally vulnerable to the type of narrative warfare practiced by Russia. As we have seen, especially during the 2016 election cycle, narratives are a particularly difficult type of propaganda/ influence to resist. This is because narratives trigger audiences based on their unique narrative identity. The only way to combat such warfare is to educate and mentor citizens regarding digital and media literacy. In other words, **the primary weapon system is narrative resilience.** This literacy must also be supported by leaders across the spectrum of society. The U.S. also must rekindle its relationship with its own unique national narrative that solidifies our values against enemy values. We absolutely must remember that when it comes to tribal/narrative identity, the most important in warfare is national, not Republican, Democrat or otherwise. Only citizens can fight this type of foreign influence and it will require brutal honesty with ourselves. If wanting your side to "win" is your only goal, the entire nation loses.

By following these simple ideas, each and every citizen will be as qualified as our original minutemen were 249 years ago. There is every bit as much at stake now as at the founding of our nation and it's again up to us, the citizenry, to protect it. It's on you to be courageous, honest and responsible – but then again, that's what patriotism has always required.

- Fact check by way of one of the respected mainstream fact check sites.
    - Fact-check.org
    - Politifact
- As much as is reasonably possible, verify accounts in all social media platforms.
- Question each and every source.
- Always become aware of the other side of the story, not just the one that you like.
- Never hit "send" before sourcing content.
- Follow advisory sites such as "The Propaganda Critic," The Securing Democracy project.
- If a source always presents only one-sided political or social content, see this as a warning sign and seek information elsewhere to verify.
- If something triggers you emotionally (anger, sadness, revenge, etc.), it may have been designed to influence you. Be especially careful.
- Be extremely cautious of online games, quizzes or requests to forward some type of advertisement or sentiment. These are often designed to access your connections.
- Be extremely cautious of websites. Many mimics are designed to look almost exactly the same as the real thing.
- Caution friends and family when you discover dishonest content or accounts/profiles that distribute such content. Warn them that they are being targeted.
- Ensure your computer, phone and tablets have up-to-date security.

- Trust advisories from federal law enforcement and the intelligence community.
- If someone you read or follow demonstrates that they are trying to dishonestly influence you, act accordingly. Block, mute and report.
- Beware of trolls and bots.

6

Patriotism Is About Country over Party.

TAT Truth About Threats Published on Substack
August 14, 2023

Today's TAT and food for thought as you go about your week, is an intersection of the topics I talk about frequently in my TAT articles. The general categories of those topics include at a minimum:

1. **Our failures in protecting the nation from professional influencers both foreign and domestic.**
2. **The hyper-partisan nature of politics**
3. **Fundamental misunderstanding of our founding values and Constitutional principles.**
4. **Oligarchy**

There are plenty more national security threats as well, that play into the four items above, but even these four, will be challenging to get into one TAT article. Since I tend to write longer articles, today I will try and be more succinct so that the complexity of the issues does not overwhelm readers. For the record, they often tax my brain too.

1. **Our failures in protecting the nation from professional influencers both foreign and domestic.**
   a. The bottom line here is that there is no way, for the US government to effectively protect our citizenry from what is called, malign influence, or in plain language, those who wish to do our nation harm. So that I do not rehash what I have written previously on this topic, the links are below.
      i.
         1. The US National Security Community has left us a critical vulnerability in US national security. (truthaboutthreats.com)
         2. Protecting our nation from Mis and Disinformation, requires true expertise at Ethical Influence (truthaboutthreats.com)
         3. Dear America, I dare you! - by Paul Cobaugh (truthaboutthreats.com)
         4. Without a core, shared, national identity, there is no national security. (truthaboutthreats.com)
         5. Hyper partisanship will sink our Republic, especially when one side has fully abandoned honesty, integrity and morality. (truthaboutthreats.com)

The reason that this category is part of today's piece is that US citizens have been victimized by the unscrupulous and sometimes downright evil professional influencers and marketers from a variety of sources, such as:
- Political operators

- Oligarchical donors buying influence in both politics and US defense spending.
- Propaganda media like FOX, Newsmax, Breitbart, MSNBC and more
- Foreign adversaries like Russia, China, Iran, North Korea, extremist and violent extremist organizations like MAGA, AQ. ISIS, Anarchists, Boogaloo Bois, Accelerationists, pro and anti-Abortion extremists etc. Of all of these, only MAGA presents an acute national security threat now due to Jan 6th, treasonous violent extremism and their command of the House of Representatives under Speaker, Kevin McCarthy.
- CYBER operations and hackers/ mercenaries working for adversarial nations and their domestic partners.

Most of those named, use their skills to isolate and encourage dissention, often violent dissention between political parties and their supporting organizations. An example, the NRA in supplying Russian money to the Trump campaign during the 2016 election.

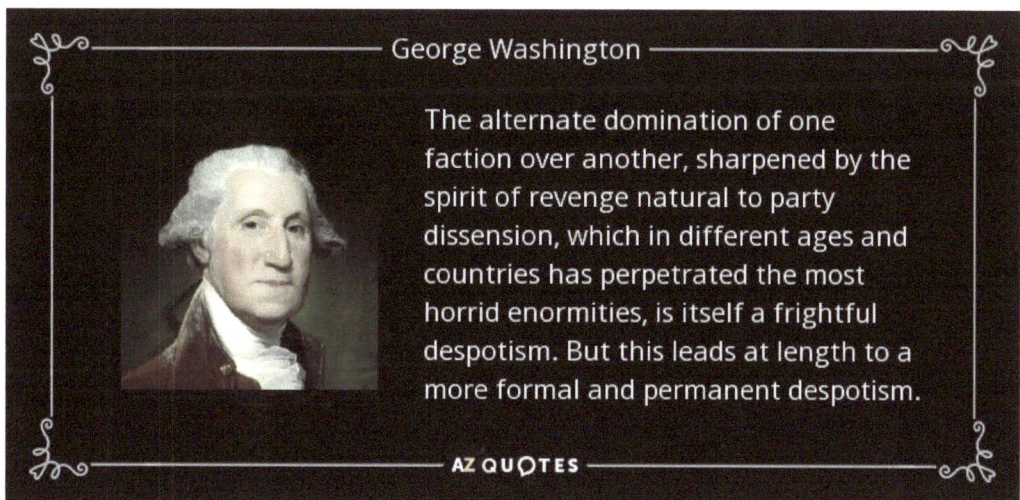

George Washington

The alternate domination of one faction over another, sharpened by the spirit of revenge natural to party dissension, which in different ages and countries has perpetrated the most horrid enormities, is itself a frightful despotism. But this leads at length to a more formal and permanent despotism.

AZ QUOTES

2. The hyper-partisan nature of politics

Our Constitution says nothing about political parties or what were often called political, "factions" at the founding of our nation. Our first and only truly independent POTUS, George Washington abhorred factions and warned decisively of the threat to our fledgling republic in his published *Farewell Address* when voluntarily leaving office after his second term. He had seen the threat by factions historically and in the eight-year timeframe since he took office as our first POTUS. He was adamant about this threat and recent events since the Trump administration, have been validated beyond challenge.

In recent years and during the Reagan administration, Newt Gingrich began the era of scorched earth politics where no compromise was acceptable. This set the style of the hyper-partisan battlefield that now perfectly describes the American political landscape. No democracy can survive such unethical and especially un-American thinking.

Trump, riding the coattails of such thinking and supported by Russia, took the 2016 election and ever since, the current version of the MAGA controlled GOP is now entirely sustained on conspiracy theories that do more for enemies like Putin, as well as American and foreign Oligarchs. They do not advance American values and our Constitutional principles at all. Read this last sentence out loud until it tastes as bad in your mouth as it does mine. Sadly, this is demonstrably accurate to anyone, not under the spell of party influencers.

3. Fundamental misunderstanding of our founding values and Constitutional principles.

Americans receive some or a great deal of public-school teaching about CIVICS, Government, and history, yet those under the spell of political parties have very different views of what our Constitutional principles are as well as what those principles mean. As the son of a history and government teaching father who had a large library at home on the subjects, my interest in such have only grown from deep interest over the ensuing years but those subjects now frame my perspectives regarding national security threats.

There is inherent danger in what most so-called "red-states" are doing over the past couple of years with their efforts to rewrite or omit history that doesn't suit their fake-patriotism agenda. In fact, their aggressive campaign for vouchers is an attempt to have the state pay for education in private schools that would be of lesser quality and permit rabid Christian Nationalism to be taught on taxpayer dollars. This is precisely the attitude of the Texas Republican Party who have ensconced such this as part of their most recent party platform. Nothing is more fundamentally unconstitutional than this.

I am not a partisan at all but work actively against concepts that constitute an acute national security threat. In this phase of US history, that means working against a GOP that has professionally skewed the definition of patriotism over nearly three decades with FOX News being the primary cheerleader for fake patriotism.

---

4. **Oligarchy**

The correlation of oligarchy to hyper-partisanship is as follows:

1. In order for a political party to have a loyal base, they must be convinced that only their party has the answers.

2. The way to convince party members of this requires influence, or in this case, professional influence operations.

3. Such influence operations, like the anti-American narrative selling done by the MAGA/ GOP influencers, requires money… lots and lots of money.

4. Oligarchs or what we used call, "captains of industry" use this to their advantage.

5. These oligarchs purchase influence in Congress that helps to keep them more profitable, pay less taxes or like big oil, buy themselves less environmental and operational interference from the US government. As a Texan, I see this every single day. Big oil operates with impunity here in the Lone Star State. Case-in-point, also why huge banks and other oligarchical persons and entities pay so little tax compared to most Americans.

To sum up today's short lesson on why and how hyper-partisanship has saddled our republic with party over country issues, it is important to remember that there are several contributing factors. The four primary factors are the ones touched upon in this TAT piece.

The most serious threat among this group of issues stem from the fake patriotism of the US MAGA controlled GOP. They have reshaped their version of American identity into something unrecognizable to true patriots. According to the GOP today, in order to be a patriot requires being a white male, carrying a gun, imposing their Christian Nationalist views on all Americans. Nothing… absolutely nothing could be further from US values as described in our founding documents, including our Constitution.

The professional influencers and other hired guns are paid for by oligarchs, foreign and domestic who pay to keep our nation, artificially divided, in order to wield influence in congress for their own selfish interests. For the record, during Soviet times and also with Putin's regime, dividing the US along existing cultural fault lines, was the primary focus of our primary adversary._Add to this that these influencers prey on American voters completely out of touch with how our republic works, and a national security community incapable of defending citizens from adversarial influence and we can all see how January 6th occurred. A party built on fake American values and a party that struggles to remain united and inspired to come out and vote, are all part of the combined effects of malign influence.

It is up to congress to begin doing their job, based on our founding principles. It is up to courts to codify those principles rather than doing what our current SCOTUS seems intent on doing, undermining those principles and what apathetic voters, swayed by conspiracy theories and wildly divergent agendas vote for. **Democracy in our republic is a team sport. When one part fails, the rest follows, unless we demand a return to what our nation was designed for.**

The bottom line: Send voters back to CIVICs class, legislate protections against oligarchical, political influence and for heaven's sake, dictate to the national security community, who is the primary reason that we've failed at defending the minds of our citizens, that it's time to stop listening to the so-called experts that have produced four decades of failure.

The Scene at the Signing of the Constitution by Howard Chandler Christy

7

Fact Checking Separates Patriots from Partisans

This chapter, based on previously published articles is a little bit how to and partly a dare, and will provoke some personal introspection. Still, it's not fair to ask for volunteers to man the parapets without some training.

The single biggest gap in US defenses about adversarial influence campaigns is mis/ disinformation. We are all now all too familiar with the term fake news. Regardless of what we call the deceptive use of information, its prior, ongoing, and yet-to-come examples have already conditioned and mislead millions of US voters.

Only individual citizens can defend what is between their own ears. The price of citizenship is that if someone votes, they have the obligation to be well and honestly informed. They owe to themselves, their neighbors, and their entire nation. Being well-informed about information is the equivalent of being well armed in regular combat. No one would consider defending their home and family by willingly choosing to be unarmed. Voting is no different.

Best of luck with this chapter.

Homeland Security Today Magazine:

Fact-Checking Separates the Patriots from the Partisans

January 20, 2020

From Merriam Webster:

Definition of partisan

A firm adherent to a party, faction, cause, or person

especially: one exhibiting blind, prejudiced, and unreasoning allegiance

Definition of Patriot

One who loves and supports his or her country.

… praised him as a … motivated patriot who was fearless in the quest to preserve American security.

— W. R. Hearst, Jr.

     Are you a partisan or patriot? It's really a very simple question that most assume they already know the answer to. What would happen if you were challenged to take a dare that is short, simple, cost and pain free in order to find out the answer? Would you do it? Granted, this dare is not easy and for the simple reason that it requires pure, personal honesty. What if I also told you that in order to protect our nation from one of its most serious national security threats, we all must take this dare? First, let me give you a little perspective about why we need all citizens to take this dare.

My profession is analyzing and recommending courses of action to mitigate threats to our national security. My specialties are the threats revolving around influence such as Russian and Chinese influence campaigns and threats emanating from all forms of extremism. In talking with a dear friend recently, I was asked; "What do you consider our number one threat"? Initially, I found this a daunting question but after long deliberation, settled on a choice that encompasses all of the significant threats to our republic. Considering I have worked on threats as diverse as terrorism, Russia, China, Iran and others, the threat I settled on surprised me significantly.

The bottom line is that I have a healthy belief in Americans being able to accomplish virtually anything, so long as we are united and apply ourselves appropriately. By default, anything that can undo our unity stands in the way of Americans employing "good ole' Yankee ingenuity" and facing down any threat or problem is our most serious national security threat. **In our current environment, what we refer to as *fake news* intentionally and unintentionally disseminated by foreign enemies and those who believe themselves patriotic is without a doubt, is the single most effective means of undoing our national unity. This, in my opinion makes fake news our primary national security threat.**

No problem or by extension, threat can be solved or mitigated while we are at odds with our fellow citizens. Our enemies understand this all too well and do all possible to unravel the tightly woven, patriotic fabric of US society with media designed to divide us. Their primary method is to use miss and disinformation as tools to divide us or as is commonly known these days as "fake news". The truth is, facts matter and more importantly, the truth that is made up by those facts matters the most. The only ingredient missing between opposing groups, political parties, ethnicities etc. is settling on a foundation of facts to any problem or threat. Like all problem solving, you cannot succeed without analysis of what is known.

Fear, stoked by our enemies by way of fake news is their weapon of choice to influence different segments of US society to distrust other segments. Russia didn't attack us because they are strong, they attacked us to weaken the most threatening of US traits, patriotism by all Americans. Most of us still remember the Cold War and how it unified us against the Soviets.

The most important weapon against enemies plying their influence against us is truth. It is truth and belief in our common values, regardless of political affiliation that threatens despotic and dangerous enemies. This article is about one way we can settle on facts to solve problems and mitigate threats… if we dare. It will take courage and honesty by everyone who considers themselves patriotic. If this is you, **you owe it to yourself and our nation to take this dare.**

How many Americans that consider themselves patriotic would be willing to take a dare to dramatically enhance national security? No, this isn't a trick question but a sincere challenge. There is no trickery, no potential injury or cost with the exception of maybe some occasional hurt feelings or minor embarrassment. It would be a dare so painfully simple but so daunting that many will not take it nor encourage others to do so. The only requirement is the courage to honestly hold yourself to the foundational standard that our Declaration of Independence is built on; that truth is "self-evident". So, what is this dare that most self-proclaimed patriotic citizens will be afraid to try?

The Dare

For 2 weeks, every single time that you post, tweet, share, re-share, retweet or something similar, you must fact check both the source and the information first. The bottom line is that you must decide if you've done all possible to share truth, facts and both in context. To keep yourself accountable, you must be willing, if challenged to look your spouse, partner, family member, friend or acquaintance in the eye and say, "I promise I have done my best to ensure this   information is correct and in context." You must also be willing to look at yourself in a mirror and swear that you've done your best. Finally, you must agree to challenge at least 3 others to take the dare.

I suppose that you are wondering how that something as simple as a **dare** could have an impact on national security and it's a very fair question. This dare is about using truth, not political bias to make decisions. We are currently plagued by so-called "fake-news" which has been politicized to the point that most voters simply disregard any information that comes from outside their "political tribe" and with equal ferocity share the opposite, regardless of whether it's true… or not. This merely keeps Americans divided, unable to come together to fight common enemies like Russia, China, Iran and others. This is precisely the intent of our enemies, to use dishonesty to prevent us from seeing that we are all in the same tribe… the American tribe. **A citizens' duty of being part of the American tribe is to protect the whole tribe, not just some subset of the tribe!**

In our republic we elect representatives as our voice. They cannot make decisions without truth. By the same token, we cannot elect the best representatives of our opinions without truth. Facts matter! The only question then is; "if facts matter, then whose facts do I use, those from my political tribe or those from another tribe? **At this point in American history, we need to reframe the question into "what are the facts that support our national tribe, not the Republican or Democratic tribe."** At the moment, far too many citizens are basing their decisions on dishonest information. Most of those I'm talking about would not agree but as that this is my profession, I can assure you that this is true. Most also would not accept this opinion from anyone outside their tribe. That's why we must challenge ourselves individually by taking this dare.

This is where our dare comes into play. Becoming tribalized or partisan occurs over your lifespan. Becoming tribal to the point of rejecting what you perceive as outside information has <u>everything to do with your personal identity and narrative</u> . In order to challenge yourself, it will take courage to be willing to literally challenge your beliefs or what I would professionally call, "your own personal narrative" if need be. The real question is; "are you willing to be honest with yourself"? If not, how can you be honest with others? As a citizen, there is an obligatory requirement to be well-informed so that you can productively support our republic.

"Convinced that the people are the only safe depositories of their own liberty, and that they are not safe unless enlightened to a certain degree, I have looked on our present state of liberty as a short-lived possession unless the mass of the people could be informed to a certain degree." --Thomas Jefferson to Littleton Waller Tazewell, 1805

Now, who is willing to continue with this dare and self-assess whether you are a patriot or a partisan? Just like the haunted house on Halloween, "continue if you dare".

Introduction and Background

For the record, I am retired Army, a political independent for decades and part of an extraordinary think/ do tank, *Narrative Strategies*. Influence, in support of national security and other efforts that support the greater good is the heart of what we do. Analysis underpins every single thing we do. Good analysis requires as much verifiable information as possible to come up with workable solutions. Great analysis requires absolute honesty with yourself about the determinations of your analysis. Professionally, I have become by requirement, a nearly obsessive verifier of information. This carries over into my personal life as well. <u>Should you consider yourself patriotic, this should apply to you too.</u>

Our nation was attacked in 2016 by influence operations devised, executed and sustained by <u>Russia</u>. Yes, they also had plenty of help domestically, both witting and unwitting. They were back in 2018 and they are working tirelessly towards influencing our 2020 election. Russia employs a variety of techniques from CYBER, miss and disinformation, false personas

153

and a great many others to achieve their goals of dividing Americans and weakening our resolve against outside enemies. All of their efforts are wrapped around a campaign of underline narrative warfare. After some success against us and many of our allies and partners in 2016 and almost non-existent deterrence from us, other nations like China and Iran have joined Russia in attacking our elections. In regard to all of the tactics Russia and others are using, we have some defensive measures to help defend us to some degree. CYBER efforts are primarily the benefactors of the defensive measures. The biggest and most severe threat though is dishonest influence to trigger designed behaviors by certain elements of US society. Simply stated, they have and continue to use influence to pit segments of US society against each other and to influence citizens to distrust our authorities. They have succeeded beyond their wildest imagination, and we are helping them every day by believing what has come to generically be called "fakes news". Even well-intentioned but poorly informed patriots will share and reshare "fake news" if it supports their political tribe or hurts tribes outside of their own. Often, we do this unknowingly simply because we didn't take the time to verify the information.

As long as we fight with each other, we cannot do a credible job of working together to protect the nation or our allies. In this regard, we must remember that our first and foremost tribal allegiance is to the nation, not our political affiliations. Yes, it is a citizen's duty to protect the nation be it in combat or through informing ourselves honestly. We often hear the expression, "country over party" and this is exactly what Russia and other enemies wish to prevent. Protecting ourselves from this type of attack is almost exclusively in the hands of each citizen that considers themselves patriotic, not the US government or any of her entities. Only we can decide what to believe or not. Yes, accepting and succeeding at this dare is the single most frightening thing possible to our enemies. Militarily they are weaker.

Their only advantage is to influence us to believe that we are weak and divided. Surely everyone remembers the old adage, "united we stand, divided we fall"? This is why accepting this simple dare personally is so important and challenging others to do so as well. Facts matter and even more than facts, the truths that facts form matter the most.

The bottom line to our national security is that <u>every one of our citizens has a duty and obligation to protect our primary tribe, our nation.</u> This comes before political allegiance. We can and must do this. We've done it before and it is part of our American DNA. For example, before WWII, we were divided but came together to fight a common enemy. We simply need to <u>refocus our allegiance to the "American tribe",</u> not the R or D tribes.

Getting At The Truth

Acquiring the truth or as close to it as possible is the point of this dare and not always as difficult as some would suggest. The real challenge and the one requiring courage is accepting the truth if it differs from the views of your tribe. Tribes are about identity and everyone and every tribe have their own different identity. Identity is at the core of narrative-centric campaigns of influence and once understood, can predictably trigger responses in those targeted. This is why the threat of narrative warfare is so dangerous if left unattended. First things first though. Let's get at the truth.

How to discover truth can occasionally be complicated but in regard to most Russian propaganda, miss and disinformation, it's often painfully easy. What follows is far from an exhaustive list of techniques for discovering the truth but more than enough to meet the requirements of accepting our dare about what is available in open source media. Being well-informed is called most often, "media literacy" and these days, it's in short supply.

I received a very insightful request from my wife a while back. Though very bright and an elementary school teacher for a long time (no, I'm not saying how long) she, along with many of her teacher friends are frustrated at how to decipher the truth about what they see in media, social included. The result is to assume that everything is dishonest. This is hardly true.

For most things a citizen must vote on there is an enormous amount of credible information at their fingertips. Citizens must learn to find this information in order to make informed decisions. Learning a thing or two about "how" is not only important to each citizen, but to our nation as a whole.

For new users to the steps below, I will towards the end of the paper offer you a short practical exercise to try out your new skills. By using a couple of these simple methods, every citizen will be far more informed, should they be courageous and patriotic enough to overcome their tribal identity affiliations when the truth doesn't support them.

Following is a short list of some of the tools that I use daily and consider very reliable. I am not insisting that you only use my tools but they are certainly valuable, free and as non-partisan as I can find. As that my profession is more along the lines of overall national security from an influence perspective, some of these tools are more focused on conflict, policy, doctrine, and law.

1. Step 1. Glance at the overall presentation of the article, meme etc. Is it sensational? Does it have a provocative headline?
   a. Articles with sensational headlines, photos or graphics tend to be far less believable, especially if the headline is provocative of some emotion like anger, frustration, sadness and especially fear. Fear is the most effective emotion to keep someone dishonestly glued to their tribal affiliations. Fear, wielded as a tool of influence by bad actors is far beyond dishonest, it is dangerous.

2. Step 2. Look carefully at the link in your browser or on your device. More importantly, check the URL carefully. Is it accurate?
   a. A favorite tactic of dishonest influencers is to very slightly alter a URL so that it appears to be a link you are familiar with. This is easy to miss so please look carefully.

3. Step 3. Check a variety of sources that evaluate media sites for their bias. There are excellent, ethical and free websites whose whole purpose is to give you a measure of the level of bias for most known websites.
   a. One of my favorites is https://mediabiasfactcheck.com/conspiracy/ . This searchable website not only evaluates news but provides a variety of other insights written in plain language that will assist in your evaluation. They grade the level of bias, tell you if the site traffics in conspiracy theories or pseudo-science and also grades reporting vs. opinion as to level of accuracy.
   b. **If a site traffics in conspiracies or pseudo-science at all, trust nothing** on the site and eliminate it from your list of sources.

c. Some sites have a moderate level of bias in their presentation and opinions yet are considered fairly accurate in regards to reporting. These are some of the most challenging sites because you must constantly be on guard.

   i. It's important to note here that it's important to know the difference between reporting and an OP-ED (Opinion of an Editor). **For the purpose of verifying information, stick with reporting only**.

d. There is always a way to find real stories. If they are true they will be on sites lightly biased but containing accurate reporting.

e. **There are also several sites that are considered neutrally biased and accurate in reporting. These should always be your first choice.**

f. Everyone has their own internal bias on some level. Everyone also prefers to read, see or hear what suits their bias. **It is a major mistake to read only what you like if you are looking for truth.**

Step 4. Now, here comes the hard part… content! As noted in step 3, everyone has some level of bias depending on the topic, issue or person. The same as some people like blue and some prefer green, we all have preferences. This is due to a long and complicated discussion about internal narratives. We'll save that for another time. Simply know that when you are looking at media, there is an internal filter, unique to you that sways your opinion. Political "tribes" have people that share many of the same layers of filters about certain topics. This is why groups can be "triggered" by well-honed narratives.

a. One of the easiest ways to determine if you need to be careful about the content is to be honest about whether or not you agree and support the content. If yes, find something credible to read that challenges that opinion. The same applies if you disagree. If you emotionally find favor with content, you have probably been triggered intentionally. If reading the same site constantly produces the same reaction, you certainly have been triggered. This doesn't mean the content is wrong, but in order to do critical analysis, you must challenge your opinions. I often read sites rated with little or no bias or agenda that I don't like or agree with. My responsibility is to decide if I don't agree because of my bias or because I legitimately have a better argument.

b. On the topic of honest content, one personal rule I follow professionally is that if I cannot find a story in either the AP (Associated Press), Reuters or in the reporting section of reliable mainstream news, I almost always discard it. Professionally, I avoid all OP-ED pages because I like to figure things out without someone else's prejudices skewing my thinking. **This is a recommended tactic** but tends to be less interesting for casual users.

Step 5. This may seem all too apparent but check the date of content. When a topic is emotionally charged, bad actors like to recirculate articles and other content that may be very old in order to trigger a reaction. This tactic has no upside to you or others trying to determine truth. An important exception to using older content is that some government reports such as CRS (Congressional Research Service) etc. have no real expiration date on certain topics.

Step 6. Verify photos. There are plenty of open source, free tools for verifying photos.

    a.   Photos are a real problem. As technology advances, what is termed "deep fakes" will become a more serious problem. Even now, there are millions of fake accounts that use stock photos on troll profiles. Also, photo-shopping a photo to make it look real is commonplace. Using simple tools can alleviate most of these problems and risks.

Are You Ready to Take the Test?

Evaluate the following links and be honest with yourself about the information contained in them by following the steps above. Jot down a simple thought about how reliable each link is.

For the purpose of demonstrating my points about tribal affiliations/ partisanship I have used a very controversial issue to show just how emotional that political and national security issues can be.

Topic: Russian attacks on the US during the US 2016 elections

The following links demonstrate a Russian, National Security, Republican and finally, a Democratic narrative. Your job is to follow a handful of basic steps to come to a conclusion about the content of each, decipher its truth (or not) and finally to consider the truth from weighing each against the other 3.

One last note before beginning, I realize this is a politically sensitive topic. The topic must be sensitive in order to test your ability to resist political tribal biases or not. I have simply chosen these links and content to test your ability to figure things out. I remind you that I have zero political agenda with this content or links.

Russian narrative: https://www.rt.com/news/473840-ukraine-election-meddling-impeachment/

US National Security narrative:
https://www.dni.gov/files/documents/ICA_2017_01.pdf

Republican narrative: https://republicans-intelligence.house.gov/news/documentsingle.aspx?DocumentID=1024

Democratic narrative: https://www.reuters.com/article/us-usa-trump-impeachment/former-trump-aide-calls-ukraine-meddling-theory-fiction-trump-would-welcome-senate-trial-idUSKBN1XV0I6

Evaluating the Challenge and Taking Action

This is the hardest part as that it will challenge your internal biases. In the next two weeks, as you evaluate stories, memes etc. that you'd like to share on social media, review your answers and then, look in the mirror and see if you can honestly say out loud, "this content and website is worthy of sharing with other patriotic citizens". Finally, if you wish to continue and for extra credit, (warning, it's addictive) find credible websites that you can use to dig into the real overall truth using the same steps.

Remember, if you have honestly followed the steps, sharing content means you are either knowingly telling the truth or lying to your family, friends, co-workers, and fellow citizens depending on what you determined by following the steps. Whatever you decide to do, your conscience will guide you. Research shows that most people will not willingly lie to their family and friends, especially if they can be shown as being responsible for a post, tweet or other. Think about it, if most Americans would simply take this dare, we as a nation will make decisions based on truth rather than what dishonest manipulators like Russia would have us believe.

Just because you belong to a political tribe, it doesn't mean that the tribe is always telling you the truth whether it be intentionally or unintentionally. The essence of freedom in our republic is that we participate in our government. Wouldn't everyone be better off if we could depend on every citizen to seek truth before deciding what affects us all?

When we were attacked at Pearl Harbor at the beginning of WWII, Americans of all political persuasions banded together to conquer Fascism. During the Cold War we did the same to conquer communism. Russia and others are now attacking us daily through dishonest influence. Isn't it about time we revisit our history of functioning as one tribe, the American tribe to resist our enemies? Republicans, Democrats, Independents and others are sub-components of our primary tribe as US citizens. We can fight amongst ourselves later but first we must fight our adversaries together.

Being honest with yourself with regard to sharing information is the first step in uniting for our common defense. Now… please, take the dare and encourage others to do so. Remember, **being a patriot means being a well-informed citizen** that is courageous enough to change their mind if truth demands it.

8

Conclusions and Recommendations

A List of "Must Do" Items

1. *Build resilience in US audiences that aids in recognizing and resisting influence.*
2. *Apply CYBER tools proportionately, both offensively and defensively.*
3. *Regularly disseminate effective alternate and counter-narratives.*
4. *Message by all available and appropriate means, messaging in support of our narrative strategy.*
5. *Deterrence or rather: Demonstrate by action that aggression will be firmly resisted.*

Think of the recommendations as a "game plan" for defending our election. No matter how well soldiers are trained, success depends on a plan, leadership and so many more things. The US government is providing much of what is required under #2 and a limited amount of #5. Yes, you guessed it; it's up to dedicated patriots to do the rest. To say I am disappointed in the US government at this point would be an accurate, yet unproductive observation. In the vein of the old saying; "play the hand you're dealt", it's time for all patriots to stop complaining and get serious about our defense.

The 5 points from chapter one were published over 2 years ago and yet are little improved regarding preparedness. No problem though; US citizens, historically have never failed to rally to the defense of our nation and I don't believe we will fail in November. This book, as I am sure everyone realizes by now is oriented towards helping everyone from an everyday citizen to a national security professional organize for our defense. Simply put, if we can at least do these 5 things well, we won't fail.

There is no point in rehashing everything from chapter 1 but let's take a short look at how to go about proficiency in our strategy. First and foremost, national security is a team effort. Everyone matters and we need leaders who understand our "game plan" and know how to inspire supporting players to their best efforts. There are countless volumes written on leadership but the bottom line is, in dire situations, leaders tend, like cream to come to the surface. Inspired and proficient men and women with specific talents for leadership will step up and it's important to recognize and support them.

Petty differences must be put aside in order for leaders who've stepped up, to lead to their fullest potential. Since the biggest divisiveness in the US is political, put aside your Republican and Democratic identities and become what you should have always been first, citizens. There will always be time for debate once the battles are over but during combat, all that matters is working together.

The reason that resilience is the first point on the list, it is the most important. None of the other 4 points can succeed without resilient players. The most important part of resilience is courage. In putting aside political differences, it takes courage to deal with truth, the whole truth and nothing but the truth. Learning how to acquire such truth not only requires courage from chapter 6 but the skills from chapter 7.

When it comes to the points 3 and 4 of our game plan, every single voter is a capable disseminator of narratives and truth. If you've accomplished the courage to understand truth, it's but a small step to share it, even among family and friends that may not wish to hear it.

Finally, in this short chapter, is deterrence, point #5. Every tweet, post, engagement with the full truth is deterrence. In military terms, if an adversary encounters significant resistance, they try something else. Dispelling fake news and mis/disinformation equates to resistance. Also, under the topic of deterrence means taking action that induces costs on the adversary (s). US CYBER has this capability and have developed more since the fiasco of 2016. If they do their job and impose costs on Russia, China and others, it will diminish the will and effectiveness of the bad guys.

Ultimately in this conclusion it's imperative to say something about our domestic bad guys. There are numerous US citizens that wittingly and unwittingly support the influence assaults of our enemies by sharing dishonest content. Those who've been influenced to help our adversaries are our most serious threat and one, not easily dealt with for reasons too numerous to discuss in this book. The only alternative to dealing with these witting and unwitting citizens is for other US citizens to recognize them, mentor them if possible, call them out and/ or report them.

The two most important weapons in the hands of US patriots for the 2020 election are courage and media literacy. There is simply no excuse for citizens to not contribute to our defense. There is no cost other than the small amount of time invested in media literacy. Most of the basic tools for media literacy can be found in the annex titled, *Election Security Resources,* in the next section. Fact-checking literally takes a minute or two if the subject is more complex.

By now, as readers approach the end of this book, you should have a relatively sound understanding of the threat against the US for our upcoming election. The threats are real as we've seen before and will continue in more aggressive forms until we as a nation mount a serious defense.

As discussed in chapters 1 and 3, the US government is not up to the standards necessary outside of the CYBER realm. Dishonest influence of American citizens is our number one most serious gap in our defense. Only an overwhelming number of honest, engaged, media literate and courageous citizens can plug the defensive gap of adversarial influence.

As I close out this book, it's important that I leave you with a little of my inspiration for writing this. Like most of my generation, raised in the post WWII and Korean War era, I was immersed in the patriotic reverence for our system of government and its potential for good in the world. Mom was a Republican and Dad a Democrat. Both were as honest as the day is long and had put "their money where their mouth was" as veterans of the Korean War. Winning for a party was not their goal. Winning was defined politically as what was best for the country. Facts mattered always and one of their favorite sayings was "if you have to lie about your beliefs to win an argument, you probably should think about changing your beliefs."

Well, my fellow citizens, one of my most staunch beliefs about my patriotic duty is that we, not our adversaries should determine our future at the ballot box. If we don't, we no longer have a republic. We now know with no uncertainty that in 2016, Russia played a significant role in our elections. I and the other patriotic Americans deeply object to them or anyone else, doing this again. This book doesn't favor a party or candidate. It is precisely about the integrity of our electoral system and defending it.

As the introduction implies, every patriotic citizen must become a modern day "Minuteman" if we are to succeed in securing our elections from foreign and domestic, illegal influence. This is a good news/ bad news story. The bad news is that we live in a world where we must prepare for these types of threats. The good news is that patriots have sprung to action every time our nation was threatened. Like before WWI and WWII, we are going to war unprepared but depending on citizen soldiers to make the difference. If tradition holds, we'll be safe; but only if there are millions, not dozens of modern-day Minutemen.

Appendix

Election Security Resources

At ***Narrative Strategies***, our core competency is influence, both offensive and defensive in support of national security and projects/ programs for the greater good. Our 2020 elections are on the near horizon and from a national security perspective, still relatively unprotected from foreign influence. For this reason we have decided to do our part and add this page to our website as a **free, no subscription required source** for content and resources of value to both national security professionals and average voters.

We learned a painful lesson in 2016 regarding foreign and related unethical influence which impacted our American birthright of free and fair elections. Although some natsec progress has been made in regard to CYBER issues, the issue of American voters being influenced unethically and, in some cases, illegally during this election has not been addressed.

Strengthening resolve to influence is called resilience.

We encourage government and organizational leaders at the local level and especially individual citizens to take advantage of these resources in order to strengthen their communities. Finally, please do not hesitate to contact us if we may be of any assistance to make your communities more resilient.

How to Use These Resources

These resources currently include the following type websites and content but will be expanded as valuable additions become available.

- Fact-checking sites
- Media bias checkers
- Multi tool sites
- Educational sites
- Image verifying sites
- The official **FBI** site, *Protected Voices*
- The official **DHS** site of election resources
- Articles from National Security experts at GTSC Homeland Security Today that put the threats into perspective.

Fact Checking sites:

- https://research.library.gsu.edu/c.php?g=621030&p=4423669
- https://www.factcheck.org/
- https://www.politifact.com/
-

Media bias checker:

- https://mediabiasfactcheck.com/conspiracy/
-

Multi tool sites:

- https://blog.library.gsu.edu/2017/02/21/what-do-the-people-really-think/
- https://www.bellingcat.com/

- https://www.journaliststoolbox.org/2019/11/29/urban_legendsfact-checking/
- https://firstdraftnews.org/
- https://journalistsresource.org/tip-sheets/reporting/tools-verify-assess-validity-social-media-user-generated-content/
- https://researchguides.journalism.cuny.edu/c.php?g=547454&p=4256116
- https://libguides.valenciacollege.edu/c.php?g=612299&p=4254373
- https://libguides.lmu.edu/c.php?g=595781&p=4121899
- https://www.prattlibrary.org/research/tools/index.aspx?cat=90&id=4735
- https://archives.cjr.org/the_news_frontier/best_practices_for_social_medi.php

Educational sites:

- https://www.courts.ca.gov/documents/BTB24-PreCon2G-3.pdf
- https://www.allsides.com/unbiased-balanced-news
- https://propagandacritic.com/

Image verification checkers:

- https://www.politifact.com/personalities/viral-image/
- https://www.commonsense.org/education/videos/how-to-use-google-reverse-image-search-to-fact-check-images
- https://debunkingdenialism.com/2017/08/21/fact-checking-photos-in-4-easy-steps/

- https://www.poynter.org/fact-checking/2019/these-misleading-images-got-more-engagement-on-facebook-than-their-fact-checks/

Official FBI page: *Protected*

Voices: https://www.fbi.gov/investigate/counterintelligence/foreign-influence/protected-voices#Videos

- The FBI's Protected Voices initiative provides tools and resources to political campaigns, companies, and individuals to protect against online foreign influence operations and cybersecurity threats.

- Protected Voices resources include information and guidance from the FBI, the Department of Homeland Security (DHS), and the Director of National Intelligence (DNI).

The Threat

- Foreign adversaries, including Russia and China, and foreign-aligned groups try to illegally influence American political processes. Three common foreign influence methods are:

- Cyberattacks against political campaigns and government infrastructure. These attacks might include foreign adversaries hacking and leaking sensitive information from computers, databases, networks, phones, and emails.

- Secret funding or influence operations to help or harm a person or cause. Tactics include political advertising from foreign groups pretending to be U.S. citizens, lobbying by unregistered foreign agents, and illegal campaign contributions from foreign adversaries.

- Disinformation campaigns on social media platforms that confuse, trick, or upset the public for example, a foreign group may purposefully spread false or inconsistent information about an existing social issue to provoke all sides and encourage conflict.

The Defense

- Protect your voice. The FBI, in partnership with DHS and the DNI, have released several short videos on critical cybersecurity and foreign influence topics. The below videos include information on foreign influence tactics as well as tips and best practices on how to protect your digital devices, social media accounts, and private information from cyberattacks. New and updated videos for the fall of 2019 include:

- <u>Message from FBI Director Christopher Wray</u>
- <u>Business Email Compromise</u>
- <u>Cloud-Based Services</u>
- <u>Foreign Influence</u>
- <u>Passphrases and Multi-Factor Authentication</u>
- <u>Ransomware</u>
- <u>Router Security</u>
- <u>Social Media Literacy</u>
- <u>Supply Chain</u>

- We also encourage U.S. citizens working in critical infrastructure sectors to join InfraGard, an FBI-sponsored public-private partnership that offers the latest intelligence bulletins on cybersecurity and other threats.

We also encourage U.S. citizens working in <u>critical infrastructure sectors</u> to join <u>InfraGard</u>, an FBI-sponsored public-private partnership that offers the latest intelligence bulletins on cybersecurity and other threats.

Additional Resources

- Protected Voices Flyer and Video Guide | Voces Protegidas Folleto y Información en Español
- Election Security - Department of Homeland Security
- Elections as Critical Infrastructure - U.S. Election Assistance Commission
- National Initiative for Cybersecurity Education - National Institute of Standards and Technology
- Securing Elections - National Association of Secretaries of State
- Handbook for Elections Infrastructure Security - Center for Internet Security
- Tips for Non-Technical Computer Users - US-CERT
- OnGuard Online - Federal Trade Commission
- Stay Safe Online - National Cybersecurity Alliance
- Know the Risk, Raise Your Shield - National Counterintelligence and Security Center
- Cybersecurity - Department of Justice
- Foreign Threats to U.S. Elections (pdf) - National Counterintelligence and Security Center
- Election Security - CISA

DHS Site: Election Security Resource

Library: https://www.dhs.gov/publication/election-security-resource-library

Below is a collection of the publications and materials developed to support state and local officials in their efforts to safeguard election systems. Beyond these resources, CISA offers voluntary and free assistance to state and local election officials and authorities to support their infrastructure's security.

Checklists and Guides

DHS Campaign Checklist

A one-page cybersecurity checklist to support political campaigns in protecting against malicious actors.

Election Security Resources Guide

A compilation of CISA contacts and resources available to support state and local election officials.

HTTPS

An overview of Hyper Text Transfer Protocol Secure (HTTPS), which is used to encrypt and securely transmit information between a user's web browser and the website they are connected to. Encryption is especially important on webpages that collect information through forms or require a user to login, such as online voter registration.

Incident Handling Overview for Election Officials

A summary of CISA's cyber incident response team services for election officials as well as one page guidance on incident response planning considerations, a checklist for requesting assistance, the incident response process and common mistakes to avoid.

Protected Voices

The Federal Bureau of Investigation (FBI) Protected Voices initiative is designed to mitigate the risk of cyber influence operations targeting U.S. elections. As part of the initiative, FBI offices are coordinating with political campaigns at the local, state, and federal levels across the country to make them aware of potential cybersecurity vulnerabilities. The Protected Voices website includes resources, information and guidance from the FBI, the Department of Homeland Security (DHS), and the Director of National Intelligence (DNI).

Ransomware Executive One Pager and Technical Document

An interagency guide that provides an aggregate of Federal government and private industry best practices and mitigation strategies focused on the prevention and response to ransomware incidents.

Securing Voter Registration Data

An overview of threats to voter registration websites and databases along with recommendations on how election officials and network administrators can protect and prevent the threats.

Leveraging the .gov

The .gov domain is a top-level domain (TLD) that was established to make it easy to identify US-based government organizations on the internet. All three branches of the US Government, and all 50 states, and many local governments use .gov for their domains.

DMARC

Domain-Based Message Authentication, Reporting and Conformance (DMARC) is an email authentication policy that protects against bad actors using fake email addresses disguised to look like legitimate emails from trusted sources. DMARC makes it easier for email senders and receivers to determine whether or not an email legitimately originated from the identified sender. Further, DMARC provides the user with instructions for handling the email if it is fraudulent.

Multi-Factor Authentication

Multi-factor authentication (MFA) is a layered approach to securing data and applications where a system requires a user to present a combination of two or more credentials to verify a users identify for login. MFA increases security because even if one credential becomes compromised, unauthorized users will be unable to meet the second authentication requirement and will not be able to access the targeted physical space, computing device, network, or database.

Ransomware Guidance for Election Officials

This document includes best practices to protect your systems and data against ransomware, planning for a ransomware incident, recovering from a ransomware attack, and CISA services and support.

U.S. Electoral Process Infographic

An infographic that outlines pre-election, election day, and post-election activities that rely on election infrastructure.

Ensuring and Securing Your Vote - National Audience

An infographic outlining best practices for voters, co-logoed by the U.S. Election Assistance Commission, the National Association of Secretaries of State, the National Association of State Election Directors, and the Department of Homeland Security.

Ensuring and Securing Your Vote - State & Local Audience

An infographic outlining best practices for voters that can be customized with a state or local website for additional information, co-logoed by the U.S. Election Assistance Commission, the National Association of Secretaries of State and the National Association of State Election Directors.

Foreign Interference Taxonomy

181

An infographic that explains malign actions taken by foreign governments or foreign actors for the purpose of undermining the interests of the U.S. and its allies.

Flyers

Before You Vote - National

A joint flyer produced by the U.S. Election Assistance Commission, the National Association of Secretaries of State, the National Association of State Election Directors, and the Department of Homeland Security to educate voters on actions they should take before Election Day.

Before You Vote - State and Local

A joint flyer produced by the U.S. Election Assistance Commission, the National Association of Secretaries of State, and the National Association of State Election Directors that can be customized with a state or local election information website to educate voters on actions they should take before Election Day.

Vote with Confidence

A joint flyer produced by the U.S. Election Assistance Commission, the National Association of Secretaries of State, the National Association of State Election Directors, and the Department of Homeland Security to help voters cast their ballots with confidence.

State & Local Official Results

A joint flyer produced by the U.S. Election Assistance Commission, the National Association of Secretaries of State, the National Association of State Election Directors, and the Department of Homeland Security to remind voters that only state and local election officials provide official results.

Reports

Election Infrastructure Security Funding Considerations

A report produced by the Election Infrastructure Subsector Government Coordinating Council to provide direction to the election community regarding possible consideration, both short and long term, for the use of 2018 Congressionally appropriated election funding, as well as to provide support for procurement decisions regarding use of the funding.

Best Practices for Continuity of Operations

A paper providing organizations recommended guidance and considerations as part of their network architecture, security baseline, continuous monitoring, and Incident Response practices in order to actively prepare for and respond to a disruptive event such as destructive malware.

Topics:

- Election Security
- Collections:
- Fact Sheets,
- Infographics,
- Posters

Election Security Resources GuidePDF1.35 MB

U.S. Electoral Process InfographicPDF386.1 KB

The Ransomware Executive One-Pager and Technical DocumentPDF782.4 KB

Election Infrastructure Security Funding ConsiderationsPDF435.61 KB

Securing Voter Registration DataPDF480.31 KB

Best Practices for Continuity of OperationsPDF548.06 KB

HTTPSPDF377.57 KB

Incident Handling Overview for Election OfficialsPDF1.64 MB

Ensuring and Securing Your Vote - National AudiencePDF527.2 KB

Ensuring and Securing Your Vote - State & Local AudiencePDF413.26 KB

DHS Campaign ChecklistPDF629.2 KB

Foreign Interference TaxonomyPDF797.37 KB

Before You Vote- NationalPDF1.01 MB

Before You Vote- State and LocalPDF1003.18 KB

Vote with ConfidencePDF322.37 KB

State & Local Official ResultsPDF672.42 KB

Leveraging the .govPDF205.15 KB

DMARCPDF183.76 KB

Multi-Factor AuthenticationPDF180.53 KB

Ransomware Guidance for Election OfficialsPDF290.02 KB

Articles from <u>GTSC Homeland Security Magazine</u>, National Security experts regarding ES (Election Security), influence and narrative warfare

- Threat to the ballot box
- Homeland Security Experts on the Biggest Threats and Challenges the U.S. Faces in 2020
- Fact checking separates Patriots from Partisans
- Everyone must be a Modern-Day Minuteman to protect our elections
- Anatomy of Narrative Warfare and Social Media Ops Since the Last Election
- A Five-Point Strategy to Oppose Russian Narrative Warfare
- A simple explanation of Narrative Warfare
- The Election Official's Handbook: Six steps local officials can take to safeguard America's election systems

Select Bibliography

A. J. (2019, January 11). *The politics of fear: How fear goes tribal, allowing us to be manipulated.* Retrieved from The Conversation: http://theconversation.com/the-politics-of-fear-how-fear-goes-tribal-allowing-us-to-be-manipulated-109626

Aftergood, S. (2018, APR 30). *Strategy, directing the instuments of national power.* Retrieved from fas.org: https://fas.org/blogs/secrecy/2018/04/strategy-jcs/

Assessing Russian Activities and Intentions in Recent US Elections. (2017, January 06). Retrieved from dni.gov: https://www.dni.gov/files/documents/ICA_2017_01.pdf

Association, A. P. (n.d.). *The road to resilience.* Retrieved from http://www.apa.org/helpcenter/road-resilience.aspx

Background to "Assessing Russian Activities and Intentions. (2017, Jan 6). Retrieved from DNI.gov: https://mailchi.mp/thesoufancenter/what-protests-in-the-united-states-have-in-common-with-protest-movements-worldwide?e=4de95f5471

Bale, G. A. (2009). *Where the Extremes May Touch: The Potential for Collaboration Between Islamist, Right- and Left-Wing Extremists.* Retrieved from START UMc: https://www.start.umd.edu/research-projects/where-extremes-may-touch-potential-collaboration-between-islamist-right-and-left

Berk, A. W. (n.d.). *The Strategic Communication Ricochet: Planning Ahead for Greater Resiliency.* Retrieved from The Strategy Bridge: https://thestrategybridge.org/the-bridge/2018/3/7/the-strategic-communication-ricochet-planning-ahead-for-greater-resiliency?lipi=urn%3Ali%3Apage%3Ad_flagship3_detail_base%3B KfHKLWycSiOA3m0NPyrX%2BA%3D%3D

Bur, J. (9, Aug 2019). *State Department struggles after hiring freeze.*
Retrieved from federaltimes.com:
https://www.federaltimes.com/management/hr/2019/08/09/state-
department-lost-critical-staff-in-the-recent-hiring-freeze/

Cobaugh, C.-a. P. (2017). *Soft Power on Hard Problems.* Hamilton
Publishing.

Cobaugh, P. (2017, August 12th). *Who we are as a nation.* Retrieved from
Medium: https://medium.com/@paulcobaugh/these-days-you-might-
say-that-story-telling-or-narrative-is-my-trade-79aaf1acfa9f

Cobaugh, P. (2018, October 30). *Anatomy of Narrative Warfare and Social
Media Ops Since the Last Election.* Retrieved from HSTODAY:
https://www.hstoday.us/subject-matter-
areas/cybersecurity/perspective-anatomy-of-narrative-warfare-and-
social-media-ops-since-the-last-election/

Cobaugh, P. (2018, February 27). *Narrative primer for understanding the
power of narrative as the core tool of influence.* Retrieved from
Medium: https://medium.com/@paulcobaugh/narrative-primer-for-
understanding-the-power-of-narrative-as-the-core-tool-of-influence-
c6710f4a2553

Cobaugh, P. (2018, May 14). *PERSPECTIVE: A Five-Point Strategy to
Oppose Russian Narrative Warfare.* Retrieved from Homeland
Security Today: https://www.hstoday.us/subject-matter-
areas/cybersecurity/five-point-strategy-oppose-russian-narrative-
warfare/

Cobaugh, P. (2018, October 30). *PERSPECTIVE: Anatomy of Narrative
Warfare and Social Media Ops Since the Last Election.* Retrieved
from Homeland Security Today Magazine:
https://www.hstoday.us/subject-matter-

areas/cybersecurity/perspective-anatomy-of-narrative-warfare-and-social-media-ops-since-the-last-election/

Cobaugh, P. (2019, Dec 3). *A few valuable tools for open source verification.* Retrieved from Medium: https://medium.com/@paulcobaugh/a-few-valuable-tools-for-open-source-verification-9ee6e2f4aecd

Cobaugh, P. (2019, January 21). *Narrative Warfare.* Retrieved from Medium: https://medium.com/@paulcobaugh/narrative-warfare-14ab7fa7ef89

Cobaugh, P. (2020, April). *Ethical Influence, the broken down rusting vehicle of America Power.* Retrieved from Narrative Strategies.com: https://www.narrative-strategies.com/failed-usg-influence

Cordesman, A. (2020, Feb 13). *The FY2021 U.S. Defense Budget Request: A Dysfunctional Set of Strategic Blunders.* Retrieved from CSIS: The FY2021 U.S. Defense Budget Request: A Dysfunctional Set of Strategic Blunders

Coutu, D. (2008). *Smart Power.* Retrieved from Harvard Business Review: https://hbr.org/2008/11/smart-power

Disinformation, Fake News and influence campaigns of Twitter. (2019, Oct). Retrieved from The Knight Foundation: https://kf-site-production.s3.amazonaws.com/media_elements/files/000/000/238/original/KF-DisinformationReport-final2.pdf

Fridman, O. (2017, Spring). *STRATCOM COE publications* . Retrieved from STRATCOM COE: https://www.stratcomcoe.org/ofer-fridman-russian-perspectiveon-information-warfare-conceptual-roots-and-politicisation-russian

Giles, K. (n.d.). *The Next Phase of Russian Information Warfare.* Retrieved from STRATCOM COE: https://www.stratcomcoe.org/next-phase-russian-information-warfare-keir-giles

Hoffman, B. (2019, MAR 22). *The Twin Hatreds.* Retrieved from Washinton Post: https://www.washingtonpost.com/news/posteverything/wp/2019/03/22

/feature/how-white-supremacy-and-islamist-terrorism-strengthen-each-other-online/?noredirect=on&utm_term=.377d4535500e

Homeland Security Experts on the Biggest Threats and Challenges the U.S. Faces in 2020. (2020, January 28). Retrieved from HSToday: https://www.hstoday.us/subject-matter-areas/airport-aviation-security/homeland-security-experts-on-the-biggest-threats-and-challenges-the-u-s-faces-in-2020/

Human Factors/ Behavioral Science Division, C. I. (2010, April). *U.S. Polls: Public Opinion and Right-Wing Extremis*. Retrieved from START, UMd: https://www.dhs.gov/sites/default/files/publications/OPSR_TP_START_Research-US-Public-Opinion-Right-Wing-Extremism-Report_Apr2010-508.pdf

Jefferson, T. (1789., Jan. 8). *Thomas Jeffereson to Richard Price*. Retrieved from Library of Congress: https://www.loc.gov/exhibits/jefferson/60.html

Johnson, T. (2019, FEB). *Taliban Narratives: The Use and Power of Stories in the Afghanistan Conflict*. Retrieved from Oxford Scholarship Online: https://www.oxfordscholarship.com/view/10.1093/oso/9780190840600.001.0001/oso-9780190840600

Lydia Kostopoulos, P. (2018, April 3-6). *Cyber Military Education in an Era of Change NATO presentation.* Retrieved from LinkedIn slideshare: https://www.slideshare.net/lkcyber/cyber-military-education-in-an-era-of-change?trk=v-feed

Maan, A. P. (2018). *Narrative Warfare, Primer and Study Guide*. Retrieved from Amazon: https://www.amazon.com/Introduction-Narrative-Warfare-Primer-Study-ebook/dp/B07S721KD3

Malcher, A. (2015, May 10). *Russian Spetsnaz – Ukraine's Deniable 'Little Green Men'*. Retrieved from Modern Diplomacy: https://moderndiplomacy.eu/2015/05/10/russian-spetsnaz-ukraine-s-deniable-little-green-men/

Mueller, R. (2019, March). *justice.gov*. Retrieved from Report On The Investigation Into: https://www.justice.gov/storage/report.pdf

Munoz', A. P. (2012, APR 30). *The Imperative of Doctrine Harmonization and Measures of Effectiveness*. Retrieved from RAND: https://www.rand.org/pubs/research_briefs/RB9659.html

ORDWAY, D.-M. (2020, Jan 10). *"Rated false": Here's the most interesting new research on fake news and fact-checking*. Retrieved from NiemanLab: https://www.niemanlab.org/2020/01/rated-false-heres-the-most-interesting-new-research-on-fake-news-and-fact-checking/

Paul Cornish, J. L.-F. (2011, SEP). *Strategic Communications and national strategy*. Retrieved from Chathamhouse.org: https://www.chathamhouse.org/sites/default/files/r0911es%E2%80%9 3stratcomms.pdf

Ph.D., D. R. (2018, June 18). *Tribalism in Politics*. Retrieved from Psychology Today: https://www.psychologytoday.com/us/blog/bias-fundamentals/201806/tribalism-in-politics

Polyakova, A. (2018, March 20). *The Next Russian Attack Will Be Far Worse than Bots and Trolls*. Retrieved from The Lawfare blog: https://lawfareblog.com/next-russian-attack-will-be-far-worse-bots-and-trolls

Polyakova, A. (2019, July 10). *US efforts to counter Russian disinformation and malign influence*. Retrieved from brookings.edu: https://www.brookings.edu/testimonies/u-s-efforts-to-counter-russian-disinformation-and-malign-influence/

Rathje, S. (2018, Dec 12). *Do we need a common enemy?* Retrieved from
Psychology Today: https://www.psychologytoday.com/us/blog/words-
matter/201812/do-we-need-common-enemy

Rosenwald, M. (2017, FALL). *Making media literacy great again.* Retrieved
from Columbia Journalism Review:
https://www.cjr.org/special_report/media-literacy-trump-fake-
news.php

*RUSSIAN ACTIVE MEASURES CAMPAIGNS AND INTERFERENCE IN
THE 2016 ELECTION VOL 1 of 5.* (2018). Retrieved from
intellignence.senate.gov:
https://www.intelligence.senate.gov/sites/default/files/documents/Repo
rt_Volume1.pdf

Simple Sabotage, Field Manuel. (1944, JAN 17). Retrieved from CIA.gov:
https://www.cia.gov/news-information/featured-story-archive/2012-
featured-story-archive/CleanedUOSSSimpleSabotage_sm.pdf

Strategic Communication; JOINT operating concept. (2009, OCT 7).
Retrieved from www.jcs.mil:
https://www.jcs.mil/Portals/36/Documents/Doctrine/concepts/jic_strat
egiccommunications.pdf?ver=2017-12-28-162005-353

Strategy. (2018, APR 25). Retrieved from fas.gov:
https://fas.org/irp/doddir/dod/jdn1_18.pdf

Summary of the National Defense Strategy. (2018). Retrieved from
dod.defense.gov:
https://dod.defense.gov/Portals/1/Documents/pubs/2018-National-
Defense-Strategy-Summary.pdf

THE CONDUCT OF INFORMATION OPERATIONS. (2018, OCT).
Retrieved from FAS.org: https://fas.org/irp/doddir/army/atp3-13-1.pdf

The Epic Identity of the Iliad and Odyssey: Pindar and Herodotus' Lofty Legacy. (n.d.). Retrieved from Center for Hellenic Studies, Harvard University: https://chs.harvard.edu/CHS/article/display/5857

Three levels of War. (1997). Retrieved from www.cc.gatech.edu: https://www.cc.gatech.edu/~tpilsch/INTA4803TP/Articles/Three%20Levels%20of%20War=CADRE-excerpt.pdf

Todd C. Helmus, E. B.-B. (2018, April 21). *Russian Social Media Influence.* Retrieved from RAND: https://www.rand.org/pubs/research_reports/RR2237.html

Under Secretary of State for Public Diplomacy and Public Affairs. (2020). Retrieved from State.gov: https://www.state.gov/bureaus-offices/under-secretary-for-public-diplomacy-and-public-affairs/

US Information Agency. (n.d.). Retrieved from This web site is an archive of the former USIA site as it stood in September 1999, and is now maintained as part of the Electronic Research Collection of historic State Department materials by the federal depository library at the University of Illinois a: http://dosfan.lib.uic.edu/usia/

US Information Agency. (2020). Retrieved from govinfo.library.unt.edu: https://govinfo.library.unt.edu/npr/library/status/mission/musia.htm

Waltzman, R. (2017, APR 27). *The Weaponization of Informaion.* Retrieved from RAND: https://www.rand.org/pubs/testimonies/CT473.html

Weaponized Narrative Initiative. (2018). Retrieved from Arizona State University: https://weaponizednarrative.asu.edu/

William S. Parkin, J. G. (2017, FEB). Retrieved from START, UMd: https://www.start.umd.edu/pubs/START_ECDB_IslamistFarRightHomicidesUS_Infographic_Feb2017.pdf

Author Paul Cobaugh retired from the US Army as a Warrant Officer after a distinguished career in the US Special Operations CT Community. During his decades long service in his expert capacity, he focused on mitigating adversarial influence and advancing US National Security objectives by way of ethical influence. He examined the centrality of influence in modern conflict, studying extremist organizations and state actors' use of influence against the US and her Allies.

At the conclusion of his military career as an influence expert, he became Vice President at Narrative Strategies, a company formed by a group scholars and military experts focused on the so called non-kinetic aspects of conflict. Paul Cobaugh collaborated with Narrative Strategies founder and CEO Ajit Maan, PhD., on *Soft Power on Hard Problems, Introduction to Narrative Warfare: A Primer and Study Guide,* and *Dangerous Narratives.*

www.ingramcontent.com/pod-product-compliance
Lightning Source LLC
Chambersburg PA
CBHW061138030426
42334CB00004B/84